Blessed To Have Received
An Offer From...

To Sue Ellen,

Thank you for all of your great energy. I am very thankful for your friendship!

Blessed To Have Received An Offer From...

A Success Manual for Student-Athletes, Their Families, and Everyone Seeking Strategies Reach Their Highest Selves

Kerry M. Sloan

Copyright © 2022 by Kerry M. Sloan.

ISBN:	Softcover	978-1-6698-1122-0
	eBook	978-1-6698-1121-3

All rights reserved. No part of this book may be reproduced or transmitted in any form or by any means, electronic or mechanical, including photocopying, recording, or by any information storage and retrieval system, without permission in writing from the copyright owner.

Any people depicted in stock imagery provided by Getty Images are models, and such images are being used for illustrative purposes only.
Certain stock imagery © Getty Images.

Print information available on the last page.

Rev. date: 02/22/2022

To order additional copies of this book, contact:
Xlibris
844-714-8691
www.Xlibris.com
Orders@Xlibris.com
838680

This book is dedicated to…

This book is dedicated to all the athletes on the journeys to making their wildest dreams come alive through the beautiful world of athletics….

I have had many people serve as amazing mentors throughout my life and for that, I am forever extremely thankful. The successes and struggles that I have dealt with as a student-athlete have molded me into the man I am today, and I am beyond thankful for the combination of all these experiences. I believe that God has put a calling on my life to serve and that was the main motivation for writing this book. No matter where you are in the recruiting process, you will find tremendous value in this book as it has been constructed to serve as a compass in the process of figuring things out. This book will be very honest and blunt at times, as I have not been known to be the most politically correct. Everything in this book derives from personal experience as a Division I, Junior College, and an All-American, All-Conference, and Conference MVP Multi-sport Division III college athlete. I earned my Bachelor of Science in Kinesiology and Sports Recreation Management and a Master's of Education in Kinesiology, and Sports Recreation Management. I also bring experiences from serving as a college football Recruiting Coordinator, a college professor, and a collegiate football coach as well.

Contents

Introduction xi
About the Author xv

PART I: HIGH SCHOOL XIX

Chapter One: Multiple Sport Participation 1
    Avoiding Burnout 1
    Reducing Overuse injuries 2
    Acceleration in The Development of a True All-Around
        Athlete 2
    Elevation Of Confidence 3
    Bryan's Story 3
    What college coaches want to know…. 4

Chapter Two: College Interest 6
    Introduction to College interest 6
        Thank God! I have been blessed to have received an
            offer from… 10
        5. Only a NCAA Division I University is giving
           out true FULL scholarship offers 10
        6. Your schooling cannot be covered unless you
           receive a full scholarship offer. 10
        7. The acceptance of an offer is not a binding
           commitment to the school, just a verbal promise. 12
        8. Most Offers Are Typically One-Year Agreements 12
    Adam Gaines Story 12
    Julie's Story 13
    Trust Yourself and Your Decision making! 15

Chapter Three: College Visits 16
    Finding The "Right Fit" 16
    In-Person and Virtual Tours 17
    The Earlier the Better 17
    What's Your Budget? 18
    Learn About the Community 18
    City area vs. Rural area 18
    Get A Student's Point Of View 19
    Check Out the Academic Departments 19

Chapter Four: "Where Are the Schools That I Want?" 21
    A Story from Coach Juice: 25
    D-I Requirements (Most difficult): 26
    D-II Requirements: 27
    D-III Requirements: 27
    NAIA 27
    College Board Sat Prep Resource 29

Chapter Five: College Commitment 30
    I've made a decision, but I think something else might
        be better… 31
    Takeaway… 32

Chapter Six: Faith 33
    Rodney's Story… 35
    The Bottom Line… 36

Chapter Seven: Leaving Home 37
    Myth #1 38
        *"I will finally be able to do what I want now, and no
        one will be able to tell me anything!"* 38
    Myth #2 40
        *Student-Athletes do worse in school than the rest of the
        student population on campus.* 40
    Myth #3 40
        *Student-Athletes are privileged and can get whatever
        they want* 40

Chapter Eight: Competition 41
    Competition: 41
    Good Competition 42
    Robbie and Janey's story: 43
    Bad Competition 43

PART II: CAN YOU TRULY B.E.L.I.E.V.E? 45

Chapter One: Build Your Foundation 47

Chapter Two: Education of Self 50
    Takeaway: 53
    Teaching yourself 54

Chapter Three: Love 55
    Jordan's Fading Passion. 56

Chapter Four: Increase EVERYTHING 60
    Question #1: 61
    Question #2: 62

Chapter Five: Energize Yourself! 63
    Natural Energy Solutions 64
    As a general statement: 64

Chapter Six: Visualization 65
    Imagine this: 65
    Scenario #2 66
    Greatness leaves clues 69

Chapter Seven: Execute 70
    Loyalty Vs. Dishonor 71
    How Can We Align Our Priorities and Our Values
        With Our Goals? 72
    Tuesday's Priority List 72
    Priority Story: 73

Chapter Eight: Rest and Recovery 75
    Make yourself a schedule 76

  JD's Story:..76
  Go to Sleep at a Consistent Time 77
  Take Naps 78

Chapter Nine: A Tale of Two Tales......................................79
  Bobby Rames (Mr. Blue Collar) 79
  Jojo (The Show) 79
  Preparation Meets Opportunity................................80

Closing Thoughts..83

INTRODUCTION

I am writing this book for the purpose of educating student-athletes and the parents of student-athletes to help give insight as to what the college athlete world is all about. Coming into college athletics as a young man back in 2010, I can honestly say that I was extremely unprepared for the life that would lie ahead of me.. This is not the case for some students, but this was my reality as a new college athlete. Although my dad was a college athlete, I was still shocked by some of the nuances of collegiate athletics, and there were different aspects that particularly intrigued me throughout my college years. The number one thing that caught my attention was the impact of the "First Generation" collegiate athlete.

Being the first one in the family to pursue something can make you feel like a "cowboy" in the non-literal sense. A lot of the time it seemed my peers would ride out over the mountain ready to attack the world only to get bombarded with 100 arrows. If you live to see another day, you are considered a pioneer and instrumental in the development of your family and community.

Thoughts on this topic are usually discussed in retrospect, from the point of view of a professional athlete. This view is not the reality that is to come for most collegiate athletes. The intent of this book is not to look down or up at the life and journey of becoming a college athlete, but rather to shed a light on the process and experiences through the eyes of myself and others that have been involved in the realm of college athletics.

I want to engage you in a journey through the eyes, hearts, and minds of the many college athletes that make the monumental decision of attacking their wildest dreams through the means of a quality education.

Through a collection of short anecdotes, principles, information, and practice you will embark on the journey of what is to come for yourself or your student-athlete as they pursue their ultimate dream of achieving a degree at the helm of a collegiate athletic experience. All stories in this text are absolutely true, I have changed the names of some of the individuals who are still involved in collegiate athletics out of respect for them and to protect their privacy. As a disclaimer, I love all of the experiences that I amassed throughout my career in collegiate athletics. I have met some of the best people I will ever meet through college football and I would not trade those experiences for anything in this world. I just wish that there had been a guide when I entered the world of collegiate athletics at the tender age of 18. I longed to know what would come along with my new experiences as a collegiate athlete and I thirsted for anything that looked like a preview.

For that athlete that feels just like I did in 2010, this book is for you. May all of your dreams and desires come to fruition and you lead a life for yourself in secondary education that makes everyone in your family proud. May you carry the values that have been instilled in you to the mountains of West Virginia or down into the sunny area of Southern California. Be brave and bold in your adventure, as it will take a strong character to be able to thrive in such a way that inspires those who wish to be in your position. As a believer in Christ as my Lord and Savior, I will say a supreme belief is paramount in regard to your navigation of the ensuing expedition that awaits you. You will experience MANY ups and downs and to be honest you will debate whether you are doing the right thing with your life at different times. Stay the course. Understand that the only way to go through something that is classified as a "hard time", is to grow through it. Grow through it all my friends. Never give up and take the journey one step at a time.

ABOUT THE AUTHOR

My name is Kerry Sloan and I hail from Harker Heights, Texas. I was born in Watertown, New York to two active-duty military soldiers to whom I give the utmost credit for the multitude of my life's personal successes. Both of them were very diligent and hard-working individuals and they instilled those qualities within me. I have a younger brother, Korey Sloan, who was born in Germany due to the traveling lifestyle most military families endure. My mother is a Jamaican immigrant who made the decision to serve her new foreign country. My father is from Chicago, Illinois and he served 20 years as an active-duty service member, also serving as a professional track athlete and coach throughout the bulk of his life. My father joined the service looking for an opportunity to work and change his life by honoring this great country. Throughout our stops as a family, we were stationed in Fort. Hood, Texas for a good amount of my life and that is where my experiences in athletics began. Throughout my childhood, there was also a brief stint in Ft. Irwin, California that I also contribute to my athletic experiences because it helped shape my understanding and gave me a more diverse perspective of athletics. My father is a hall of fame track and field athlete for DePaul University, holding the record for the fastest 400m hurdle time in their history to date. I spent a large majority of my early years on the track with my dad and trained during summers and off time from school which had a significant influence on my athletic infatuation. I grew up on track and field for a lot of my younger years which gave me a plethora of knowledge about nutrition, kinesiology, and the inner workings of athletics fairly early.

As a young man, I ran track, played football, basketball, baseball, and soccer. As time progressed, due to my athletic build (and lack of superior foot speed) I took a strong liking to football, and it seemed to be the one place that I finally felt that I "fit". This happened in fifth grade and I know that I possessed a "gift" to play the game that I quickly fell in love with.

I was a troubled child throughout these years, I was very angry as a young man and the football field allowed me a release. It was where I felt free and without the many cares that I had in the world. As I moved into high school, I played primarily football while still running track and playing basketball. Through four years I earned two scholarship offers to play during my senior year at NCAA Division II Missouri-Southern State University, then one later in my senior year at NCAA Division (I-AA) Montana State University. I made the decision to go to Bozeman, Montana as it offered me a better opportunity to go and pursue my lifelong dream of becoming an NFL running back.

I arrived at Montana State in July of 2010 to begin summer workouts with the team. I stayed away from home and built relationships with my future teammates while preparing my mind and body to play collegiate football. As the fall approached, the NCAA released information to my coaching staff that I was not deemed eligible for the upcoming season due to previous issues regarding an English course from high school. This information was released to the staff a week before our report date, so my recruiting coach and position coach worked frantically with me and my mother to get the issue resolved. With my high school counselor being thousands of miles away, documents were emailed and faxed every day from all who were involved. The process was very difficult for me as I had no idea why or what was happening. I was unable to practice with the team or even attend practice due to NCAA eligibility requirements. I was devastated. The issue was resolved three weeks into the season but I was faced with more adversity.

I was invited to a party "kickback" with a couple of the senior football players for drinks. I consumed those drinks then took the wheel. I figured since I was down the street from my dorm, I probably didn't have much to worry about but I was WRONG. I was pulled over a block away and charged with Driving Under the Influence. It was the day before our first scrimmage. I acted as if nothing happened, went to practice the next day, and played in the scrimmage the following day. I saw action throughout the first four games as a running back and special teams' player growing within my role on the team even though my role was not as significant as I would have liked. As we prepared to travel to Sacramento State to play a conference game against the Hornets I was called in to speak with my head coach. He told me that a fan from a neighboring town told him that they saw my charge in the paper and he suspended me from the Sacramento State game. It marked the end of any significant playing time for me for the rest of that year and spun me into a downward tailspin. My freshman year of college was followed by drugs, girls, and parties as I attempted to cope with the dark feelings that constantly clouded my thoughts. This led to late meetings, missed classes, failing grades, and more issues that were a byproduct of the bigger issue. As my freshman year of college ended, I had passed a grand total of three classes, and I was on academic probation. Even though I had gone through so much I vowed to myself that the new year would be different! I prepared for the upcoming season like I never had prepared before in my life, aiming to do everything with an attitude of perfection. I found my confidence and had people in my life that supported and believed in me. Wow, what a feeling! As the season began, I was in a prime position to fight for a rotating running back position. I played well and was impactful on the field until adversity struck again. On a running play to the left sideline late in a game against a lesser opponent, everything changed. The defender grabbed my legs as another player jumped on my back and I heard the scariest sound that any athlete could hear …. "Pop"! I hit the ground screaming in pain. I hopped off the field and knew something was wrong, I just didn't know what. The team doctor performed a test on my knee where he jerked my knee forward as confirmation that I had torn my anterior cruciate ligament (ACL).

Depression came back and this time it seemed to be here to stay. I fell deeper into the hole of low self-esteem and loneliness as I pulled myself from all social interaction. I was only a shell of myself, hating myself because I couldn't even take showers alone. I turned to marijuana and alcohol to cope, but that didn't work and only seemed to complicate things. I was down and out, and I couldn't find a way out. Crying myself to sleep thinking of the dreams and hopes that would never come to fruition now that this injury had just changed my life forever.

You see, this moment and more of those moments that I experienced throughout my collegiate career are why I am writing this book. This book is to support and encourage those in similar situations and anyone seeking guidance. Overcoming the helplessness you feel when you have a vision for how something is "supposed" to happen but doesn't, is a process we all experience in some way. I wrote this book to tell you that it's going to be okay! You are not defined by your sport and youre not defined by the mistakes, failures, or shortcomings you experience. You are defined by how you handle those things and you get to decide what that looks like. You have to know and remember your "why", even when it comes to college athletics. It is the only way to move forward when you feel defeated. What's your "why"?

Fast forwarding, I ended up transferring (more than once) and ended up at my alma mater Hardin-Simmons University where I graduated with a bachelor's and master's in Kinesiology and Sports Recreation Management. I NEVER intended to take that route but I am glad that I did. It aligned with the future that God had planned and put me on my path, I am grateful. The bruises and bumps I endured along the way were critical. They wounded my ego but built my character which is directly related to the success I've had. Our experiences mold us and mine made me into the man that I am now and continue to become.

PART I: HIGH SCHOOL

"High school is what kind of grows you into the person you are. I have great memories, good and bad, some learning experiences and some that I'll take with me the rest of my life." – Giancarlo Stanton

High school is an interesting time in the life of all students. The mind of a high schooler is pulled in a lot of different directions, and most of the pull factors are coming from peers. Sometimes the pull can be whether to go to the movies. Regardless of the destination, the important questions always get asked first "who is going?", "When are they going?", "can I really go?" "should I go". There is also a dark reality that parents don't want to face but it presents itself in the lives of high school students and is often a factor. A study done by National Center for Education Statics found that "students with friends who were interested in having sex, drinking, and using drugs experienced less desirable educational outcomes. These students experienced a higher rate of dropping out of school and a lower rate of being enrolled in academic programs, graduating from high school, and pursuing post-secondary education". This evidence supports the idea that what student-athletes face daily is a burden they should all be applauded for carrying. For many, the pressure can truly be a lot, for some it can be too much. That's why having a plan/vision for your future is critical. Students are less likely to engage in those activities when they have long term goals that they are working towards and looking forward to. Talking with friends, coaches, parents, and trainers about the excitement of attending college can keep student athletes motivated and is often enough to convince them to refrain from risky behaviors.

The primary thing all high school student-athletes need to know is that they should enjoy their time in high school. This will be the freest of responsibility that you will ever have. After this, your journey into adulthood will be fast and furious so get yourself ready! The best thing to do to make sure that you are getting yourself ready is to listen to your own inner voice. There are going to be a lot of people telling you about what you should and should not do, but you must always make sure to listen to yourself first. No one truly knows what you want from your life, but you so I always make sure to open any conversation with a potential collegiate athlete in that way.

You must be careful in high school because not every situation is what it seems. High school is just a very small portion of what your life will encompass. **It's very important as a student to know that the harder you work in high school, the easier life will be after high school.** No matter if you work as you should, or you lack work ethic, you will still be under-skilled and under-prepared for some of the obstacles that lie ahead. The greatest teacher will always be experienced, so you should always multiply experiences. Growing up in Killeen Texas was a very open experience. It was very important that I maintained my personal space. Keeping friends around and relationships that helped my end goal was important to securing my scholarship for my college opportunity. Towards the end of my high school career, my lack of focus ended up following me into my freshman year of college. My father kicked me out of the house the summer following my senior year. That summer I was sent to college early in June, and that should've been a benefit. Although I left early, I went to college without drive and motivation due to being homesick. Circumstances should not dictate outcomes.

Reevaluate your situation and make sure you're working 10 times harder than you think you should be. It is likely that you are not working hard enough even if you are giving ultimate effort. Things that you should be doing you should be communicating with your counselors at least every semester. You should be communicating with your coaches talking about your goals, your dreams, your aspirations. You should be communicating with your parents to find out what kind of resources you could possibly tap into notes to make you go to reality. **You should have applied for multiple scholarships by your junior year.** People paying for school represents most of the debt in this country, free school is a blessing!

Find other people who have done what you're trying to do, link up with them, take notes. Look for mentors that have done all the things you want to do and have been to the process in its entirety. Use resources such as this book to help you and guide you on the road to where you want to go. Don't feel as though you have to read this book straight through or in order. Read this from page to page, or jump to a section that you think could help you out the most right now. This is a tool for ALL student-athletes. The B.E.L.I.E.V.E strategy located in Part II of this book is a strategy that can be applied to any area of life. This book will take you to the next level, but first, we will have to start it out right!

If you are like most potential collegiate athletes, up until this point you have played a lot of sports. This should not stop here and this will be critical in your ability to be successful, as I will detail in the following chapter. The grind does not stop for those who really want the ultimate prize of being the best that they can be. That means that there will be a lot of early mornings and long nights in the process of becoming exactly who you want to become, embrace it. Staying involved with sports as a student-athlete is that 'secret sauce' that the best student-athletes know very well.

CHAPTER ONE: MULTIPLE SPORT PARTICIPATION

We are a sum of the things that we repeatedly do, so make sure that you are always not too far out of season.

Some type of sports preparation or participation should be taking place in your life during the spring, summer, fall, and winter. That is if you want to give yourself the absolute best chance to not only go to the next level but to be successful as well.

A few major reasons that you will one to compete in multiple athletic seasons are that this helps **avoid burnout, reduces overuse use injuries, better development of overall athletic ability, and a chance to skyrocket confidence**.

Avoiding Burnout

Sports should always be played first for the fun opportunities that they provide. They allow us to hang out with people that are like-minded and develop relationships within a healthy team setting. Parents should be able to see coaches as another set of leaders that can help lead their students on the path to greatness. When athletes specialize too early, sometimes the love for the *playing* part of the game can be lost. When this happens, it is very difficult to turn things around to get that fire back. The game cannot be a job, it must be someone that is enjoyed with the correct intention. Have fun and try different things so that your primary sport can stay fresh for you!

Reducing Overuse injuries

In order to help yourself develop as an athlete, and a person, you need variety within your life. You need variety in the drills that you do and the concepts that you are exposed to. Moving and doing things in the same way constantly creates stress on joints/bones. Participation in different sports allows the body to heal itself where it needs to during the various seasons of competition.

Acceleration in The Development of a True All-Around Athlete

When competing in a variety of sports, it is common that the vital movements in one sport will compliment your game in another. A great basketball player who masters the ability to rebound can add to the ability to play defense on the volleyball court. The movements have similar characteristics, but the **desired outcome is different.** This adds to your ability to practice certain skills, with different methods of execution. All sports do not provide an opportunity to advance and transfer physical skills. Sharpening the mental edge is critical as well. Athletes becoming more familiar with the competition process brings about a calm as time goes on. Learning to push yourself to the limit within a new area can be ground-breaking. It is important to understand where you are currently as an athlete, what you do naturally vs. what you need more practice with, and how interested you are in the new sport before committing to play a new sport.

Elevation Of Confidence

Athletics has always been 90% physical to 10% mental. The ability to learn how to complete short-term and then long-term goals is instrumental in the development of confidence. If I am used to dominating in one sport, but when I move to another sport, I must learn to be a role player and the work that takes requires a **fresh mindset.**

Bryan's Story

"Bryan was new at J.J. Burgess High School in South Dakota, and he was entering his sophomore year. Bryan was a multi-sport athlete throughout all of his younger years playing baseball, soccer, and basketball. When Bryan arrived in his new town at his new high school he was entering into his sophomore year and felt like he wanted to take a break from so many different sports. Bryan decided to focus on baseball and stopped participating in basketball and soccer. Bryan played pitcher for his high school baseball team in the spring only, not doing much else other than playing first base for the varsity team and going to school. Bryan was a two-time all-district baseball player before graduation, but unfortunately for Bryan, he was not getting much interest from colleges, and graduation was soon approaching. Bryan did not understand why this was happening, so he reached out to one of his teammates for some help. Bryan's teammate, Jeff, had 3 offers from D-II schools and Bryan was anxious to find out what he needed to do to start getting some attention. Jeff offered Bryan one of the college recruiter's numbers so he could chat with him about what it would take for him to receive an opportunity. Bryan texted the coach at first, but because the coach didn't answer soon enough Bryan figured that he'd call.

"Ring"

"Ring"

"Hello, this is coach Terry Brown from Southland State University."

"Hello coach Brown, this is Bryan Jones, I am friends with Jeff Loudermilk and I was curious as to if there are any openings over there at Southland State for a freshman first baseman?"

"Oh! Hello Mr. Jones, how are you? I just left your school a couple of days ago! Well, unfortunately, we are not just looking for baseball players now."

Terry thought to himself. Then since he'd already been turned down, he'd figured what did he have to lose. He might as well find out the reason why.

"Sir, if you don't mind me asking. Why wasn't I recruited? Is it because I just didn't have what it takes? My grade point average is a 3.0, I never get into trouble, and I was a two-time all-district athlete."

Coach Brown's voice suddenly lowered.

"Well to be completely honest with you Mr. Jones, we are full on our roster of baseball players now. Your friend Jeff was recruited to come here to play baseball AND run track so we will be combining scholarship money so we can best help his financial situation if he so chooses to play here."

"The track coaches are really excited about his potential as a 400m hurdler, and we are very excited about his potential on the baseball diamond."

What college coaches want to know....

College coaches want to know that they are recruiting the best athletes on campus. If you are playing one sport all year, that doesn't show that. You are forcing yourself to be stellar in that sport in order to be noticed. That is not the way that NCAA athletes are normally recruited. The more opportunities that you can take advantage of to show your overall athleticism the better. If you have never tried tennis, try it this year. If you play offensive line on the football team, but you are a little underweight, join the powerlifting team.

Don't rely on your primary sport to get you where you want to go. College coaches are looking for "athletes" in all sports so make sure you are showing that you are versatile. This will also keep you away from those negative peer groups that are not going to have the same mindset as you. If you want the goal of being a successful college athlete, you must keep that mindset and that must be your goal all of the time. The way to keep that edge is by staying involved in athletics, as much and as often as possible.

CHAPTER TWO: COLLEGE INTEREST

Introduction to College interest

High school can be crazy for a young athlete. They are athletes of extreme difference, vying for competitive positions that all are very similar in nature. Luckily, if you have proven your worth as a varsity athlete, you will be offered an opportunity to play at the next level. After becoming one of the best in your city or town, district, state, and possibly even the nation, you have a pretty good understanding that you're not just some pushover. If someone wants to compete against you, they better bring their A-game or they are likely to get embarrassed. It is not cockiness, it's confidence. You know you are one of the best because you prepare like it. You have put in the time to become as skilled as you are now. You are aware the only person that really has a remote chance of stopping you is going to be you.

They know that they can't stop you, let's be real about it. You are rushing for 150 yards a game on the football field, averaging 25 points per game on the basketball court, or leading the district in digs and kills on the volleyball court. Whatever you are doing, you are doing it and you are doing it well. The fans are there to come to see you and your team complete amazing feats together, with you being one of the captains of the ship.

Since this is now your reality, there is a likely chance that a monumental experience that could have a tremendous impact on the rest of your life will take place.

You receive your first phone call from a college recruiter. These calls come from the likes of Alabama, Texas A&M, Florida State, University of Texas, Texas Tech, or the University of Southern California (although this is not the reality for most potential collegiate athletes). You start to recognize the fact that you are a premium prospect for collegiate athletics if you at least see the dream clear enough to want it to manifest in your life. Even if you are not recruited by a school, making it onto a campus that competes in your respective sport is very likely.

This collegiate athlete near reality can make you a pioneer, leading your family to embark on a journey that could make you the first college graduate in your family. Maybe the high aspirations of you becoming a collegiate athlete could make you one of the first in your school or neighborhood to take the steps to make something like this happen.

You could also be in a situation where you are one of the many flourishing and successful student-athletes coming from your environment. Although you have seen friends, family, and peers go through the process, understand that your turn in the process is still important and if more so. No matter what schools are growing interested in giving you an opportunity to continue your education, you should always be grateful and consider all options.

Knowing friends attending the likes of Penn State, the University of Oregon, Fresno State, and others does not discredit your interest in a junior college affording you the valuable opportunity of coming in to develop. Being accepted by your peers will always be something that you will wrestle with. The status is not worth the value of your life. The decision and actions that you take regarding your collegiate decision should focus on what is best for you and your life only.

Chasing a status will detach your heart from your passion more rapidly than anything else. You lose the opportunity, miss, out on the experience, and mess up your ability to make good decisions. Recruiting is most importantly your business of you. This is the business of the next four-five years of your life. Take your time, be patient, and visit schools. **Navigate this book looking for details and inspiration to guide your way to and through the college athlete world successfully.**

Gaining college interest is very exciting, and this is probably the most desire a young woman or young man will have felt to this point. The scary part is that it is by complete strangers!

These people literally know details from your height and weight, down to the places that you go to unwind with your friends. It is the job of college recruiters to accumulate as much data on you, the student athlete, as possible. The reason for this is because there is big money in college athletics.

According to the Business Insider: "The NCAA brought in $1 billion of revenue during the 2016-2017 school year — most of which was generated by the Division I Men's Basketball Tournament, also known as March Madness."

So, the college athletes that they recruit are a big business first, so please do not be misled. Coaches will say many things to get a recruit to commit or make a decision that is in favor of the university. This happens all the time! These men and women have jobs that help them provide for their families, so the decision you make on where you will be attending school needs to be your decision!

Some coaches you meet will be genuine or seem that way, but it is always important to work with an adult when it comes to evaluating and understanding the thing that someone is telling you and whether these things represent what is best for you.

College coaches are now telling you how good you are, or you are not in some cases. Letters are coming to your house or to your school and the opportunity that was just a dream for so long is starting to feel a little real. Maybe you have been receiving so much interest that you now have offers from schools that are contacting you frequently to come and be a part of their programs through text messages, emails, letters, and phone calls. As you gain more interest from schools, always know what your <u>leverage point</u> is. **Your leverage point represents the reason(s) why a school is interested in you coming to be a part of their program.**

Leverage points can be the fact that you are a left-handed point guard with a 4.0-grade point average. You could be the tallest, most skilled volleyball player in the region, that has yet to make a commitment. Sometimes, a leverage point could just be the fact that you are the best option available for the school that is reaching out. Just have a great understanding of what your leverage points, or your strengths, are in the situation at hand when actively communicating with college recruiters. This is important to understand in order to avoid the possibility of manipulation. As a prospective student-athlete, you always want to maintain control within the situation knowing what you are bringing to the table so that lack of knowledge is not used against you.

Recruiting in 2022 almost runs parallel with social media. Once a couple of people "like" a recruit, the word spreads like wildfire that this is someone that we need to learn more about!

Therefore, athletes must not base their worth on the offers they have received. Receiving offers is a blessing, but the most important thing is that you now have access to the ability to receive a free education.

Thank God! I have been blessed to have received an offer from…

All college coaches and recruiters are chasing the next best thing. This is the reason why once you have received one offer; you can almost assure yourself that there are many more to come. Then athletes pick up their phones, log into their Twitter accounts, and type "Blessed to have received an offer by (insert name of given school)". The quote is seen all over social media by numerous student-athletes anxious to show their peers and other schools that they have been afforded an opportunity to attend a university and continue to participate in the sport that they love! This can be a beautiful time in a young athlete's life and it should be celebrated.

Let's now discuss some popular myths that currently surround the world of college athletics.

13. Only a NCAA Division I University is giving out true FULL scholarship offers

Tons of young athletes are misled by the "offer" term that is so loosely thrown around today in athletics by student-athletes, coaches, and parents. It is very important that athletes understand that just because a coach says that you have been "offered", that does not mean that you have received a fully-funded scholarship offer to go and participate in your respective sport free of debt. Even at Division I institutions some athletes still have to come out of pocket when it comes to fees for books or dorm expenses. The offer to walk-on (preferred walk-on) position is not funded at all. That is an opportunity to try out to become part of a program.

14. Your schooling cannot be covered unless you receive a full scholarship offer.

There are a lot of different situations that can take place leading you to not come out of pocket much, if at all. Academic scholarships are awarded to most students coming into college with a core GPA of 3.5 or higher. This is much different than a weighted GPA, which can actually exceed the 4.0 scale (like a 4.5 for example). There are also grants and other scholarships that you can apply for. You first are required to be deemed eligible for this money. For thousands of collegiate athletes, proper research and being proactive in looking for these applications could possibly cover up to 50% or higher in your overall tuition costs. You must be early in looking for what you can apply for since this money will run out very quickly due to the high demand. The federal and state governments are looking to give out this money to students free of charge.

These grants all have deadlines, and it is important to find out when those deadlines are. FAFSA (Free Application for Federal Student Aid) plays a very large role in the easing of financial stresses that students face paying for tuition costs and other college expenses. A very large part of the funding support that ALL students should apply for is the Federal Pell Grant. This amount of money that can be granted is dependent upon the cost of attendance at your school, your financial need, and other variables. According to Studentaid.gov, this amount of money can max out at 6,345 dollars. Again, do your research! There are plenty of ways to get your school paid for by multiple entities. Loans are another way the financial burdens of attending a school can be eased for families. The difference in these opportunities to gain funds and grants fundamentally lies in the fact they must be paid back. The government awards unsubsidized and subsidized loans that must be paid back six months after graduation at very favorable interest rates that will not change over time. These interest rates do not change over time. It is important to know that these loans will almost always require students to have a co-signer for these loans to get approved. Military family aid and work-study (on-campus jobs) can also help student-athletes regarding student aid as well.

15. The acceptance of an offer is not a binding commitment to the school, just a verbal promise.

The commitment to any offer that you have received is bound by nothing but an agreement between two parties.

The coaches' offer, nor the players receiving the offers are obligated to make good on this verbal agreement.

The **National Letter of Intent (NLI)** is the only legally binding contract between an athlete and a school. Most Letters of Intent prohibit student-athletes from attending. Other schools within the same athletic conference, as the agreed-upon school. Situations with the Letter of Intent change dependent upon the terms within the agreement.

16. Most Offers Are Typically One-Year Agreements

The blessed scholarship can be gone, quicker than it has arrived for numerous reasons. Failing classes, discipline issues, or a lack of performance could all be potential factors playing a role in losing a scholarship after a year. The players that usually occupy scholarships, have them renewed by the head coach yearly.

Adam Gaines Story

Adam Gaines never really wanted to play football. Adam played because it was an opportunity to build a relationship with his dad. He had always been a confident young man and a hard worker. Adam's grades made it to where he would not have any issues getting into most colleges. Colleges sent letters for academics, but his sights stayed tightly on the gridiron in hopes of making his father proud. The barrier that he would have to get over was his size and strength. Adam played outside linebacker standing at 5'9 weighing 185 pounds. Big Division I schools was much less than interested to find out what Adam might be capable of. Adam found a break. Making it on to a small FCS school in Georgia as a **preferred walk-on**. Adam was extremely proud of himself, and his family was excited. They held a signing day at Adam's high school, and he and his family dreamed together about what future the college ranks would hold.

Adam reported to camp in August that year to find out that being a preferred walk-on, wasn't quite what he had within his mind when he thought about playing college football. Adam felt as though he had to earn his spot every day! He always ended up playing scout team against the best players on the team, making him feel as though he wasn't put in enough situations in practice to really show what he had.

Adam received a crushing blow on a "crackback" block during a punt team period before a game, then finally decided that enough was enough. Adam worked religiously on his technique and film study following his first month on the team. Adam soon gained a level of understanding of their defense that was so vast, in the film room with his teammates, Adam knew everyone's assignments and knew when someone executed poorly. The coaches took notice and began to expand his role within the team gradually. By the end of that season, the head coach called Adam into his office to discuss his future with the team. During this meeting, the head coach let Adam know that he was being upgraded to a full scholarship!

Even though Adam did not want to play football in college, he was getting his schooling paid for fully through the program. He switched his major to biomechanical engineering and graduated with his four-year degree, **free of charge**.

Julie's Story...

"Julie Beesaw was completing her senior year of high school one year early and could not wait to start her new journey of college athletics.

Being a first-generation college student, it was very important to Julie that she made the most of her opportunity to go make her family, community, and school proud of her as she moved on to the next level of her academic and athletic career. Julie loved the game with every fiber of her being. Julie's basketball team was the best in the city of Cleveland, Ohio, and was fresh off of a state championship run. Most of Julie's teammates were being recruited by the likes of Ohio school, a D-1 Texas school, an Oklahoma University, and a few other smaller NCAA Division I schools of the same caliber. Julie did not care as much as her teammates did where she went to school, she just wanted an opportunity. Julie did not start on her basketball team and she was not very confident in her abilities as a basketball player. She was a bit undersized as a power forward, but she was very scrappy in competition, and she had the heart of a champion. When a small NAIA school located in South Dakota reached out to Julie as the season approached its brilliant end, she pounced on the opportunity aggressively.

Julie and her mother packed their bags and headed to South Dakota for a visit in the middle of May. Julie left the visit less than satisfied but detailed to her mother that since the recruiter for the university said that she was "undersized", she didn't see herself gaining much interest in any other schools soon. Julie committed to the school one day after her visit and arrived on campus to begin summer workouts in early June. Multiple schools called Julie all throughout June as she attended summer workouts to recommend her to come on a visit to check out their respective campuses, but she turned them all down due to her lack of confidence in her abilities. Not one of Julie's teammates played at a level lower than D-II in that upcoming season. Julie was redshirted that season, and due to being homesick she made the trip back home her sophomore season to attend courses at a local junior college."

Trust Yourself and Your Decision making!

Don't decide for the next four to five years of our life out of haste. This is a very important decision, and you need an enormous amount of information before knowing that you are making the best decision for your future. Confidence is key. Believe in yourself more than you ever have when it comes to recruiting because you will end up where you believe that you should. If you competed for a high school that was very successful in athletics, the chances of you being able to go to a university at the higher levels of collegiate athletics are a lot higher than an athlete who is not in your situation. Never sell yourself short, anyone recruiting you with a heart will tell you the exact same thing.

Also, if you are coming from a school that was not very successful you can make it to a higher-level university if you go about marketing yourself correctly (I will dive into this later). Never underestimate the ability that you must go out and sell your abilities and talents to college recruiters. A rule of thumb is if your teammate can do it, it is a possibility for you as well. In a lot of situations, college recruiters recruit teammates so that the player that the school really wants has someone there with them to be able to ease their transition from high school to college. Believe in yourself and you will always have a chance!

CHAPTER THREE: COLLEGE VISITS

You are now a commodity. Through your academic and athletic prowess, you have gained interest from schools, and they aim to court you giving you the best experience that their budgets can offer you.

The importance of going on a college visit is to get familiar with a school. You really want to be able to find the right fit. The right fit will make you comfortable in making the school your home for the 4-5 years, depending on your degree plan.

Finding The "Right Fit"

In order to find the best possible school for you or your student-athlete, you must be sure to have a top-five school that could be tabbed as the "best options". The "best options" list should be compiled during the freshman year of high school. Coming into high school, there should always be a "North Star" that should be leading student-athletes where they want to goal, and a "best options" list can serve as that.

After creating a "best options" list, then a plan of action detailing when to visit those colleges is important. The first actual in-person visit to an institution will have a huge impact on whether you will still want to attend, or not. Colleges can sometimes seem to offer more than they do, and some schools don't represent all the things their universities afford due to poor marketing. It is important to pick a time to head to your top five schools before your JUNIOR YEAR, in order to get a real-life experience, attached to your vision of what college looks like for you.

In-Person and Virtual Tours

Since the emergence of the global pandemic causing coronavirus, things have changed about how often schools are willing to let student-athletes on campus. The daily operations at schools look a lot different because of some of the limited staffing at these institutions.

There are options for virtual and online tours online for most schools. Some of these visits are guided and narrated.

The best way to make the best of the virtual tours is to ask multiple questions to the tour guide and the student panel, in order to get a full understanding of what the school offers, and if that is what you are looking for.

The Earlier the Better

As students get closer to the final year of high school, their schedules are filled trying to balance school and social life – all while exploring potential college campuses. At the end of your high school career, is not the best time to start making visits to schools. It is important to try and familiarize yourself with the college process as much as possible throughout your high school experience. This advice could be extended to regular students, as well as student-athletes. Make it a family outing, a hangout experience with friends, or just a getaway for yourself.

No matter how you all want to attack this, it is important to get visits started early and often to ease stress levels later. Spring Break is an excellent time to make visits to colleges that you have had your sights focused on. More opportunities lie in late summer and early fall. Coming to classes while they are already in session (late spring and early fall) also helps student-athletes get a perspective of what campus life really looks like.

What's Your Budget?

When you are building your road map of visits for the upcoming year, be sure to calculate how much you can expect to come out of pocket. Help yourself by relieving some stress by going to multiple schools in one trip, if possible. If you are invited to a school by an athletic program, most of the time they will take care of food and lodging when you get there. In the case that they don't have money on hand, plan accordingly.

Do not break the bank to visit colleges. You will have enough financial responsibility to look forward to when you step onto campus. If a college is running you over your budget, then it means it just may not be in your best interest to take a visit to that school at this time.

Learn About the Community

The first visit to a college campus should be the first time you have investigated what the community around the school is like. What are people like? What is close to the campus? Are there options available for you to eat that are close? There are multiple variants that could play a role in your quality of life that you will need to consider going into this new environment. Make sure to do a great deal of research on the community that surrounds it.

City area vs. Rural area

Do you want to be inside of the hustle and bustle of the inner downtown area? Just know that you may have to wake 2 hours before your first class to ensure that you will be on campus in a timely manner. Or maybe you would like to be in a small town away from the city where everyone knows everyone. The type of situation where there's one gas station and a supermarket in the whole town.

Get A Student's Point Of View

If you really want to see if this is the move that you want to make for the next chapter of your athletic and academic career, be sure to get to know how the students on campus see the university. It's very important to see the way they interact with one another, identify who's who, and start to envision yourself as an active member of this institution.

Good and bad will come from getting a feel for what the students think about their campus. You must keep in mind that, sometimes students may have negative things to say about a campus because no matter what school they ended up at they just aren't really fans of the college experience overall.

Student-athletes have a unique perspective on campus life than most. The side of college visits that are not talked about much is the recruiting parties, where recruits are invited to get a taste of what they will experience when they are on campus. These recruiting parties are a **MAJOR** tool that schools use to reel in top recruits that they need to come in and contribute to the culture.

Make sure you come in with values and morals intact. Don't allow a big budget-created party culture and over hype energy for fun, sways you to choose a school that you wouldn't normally have chosen otherwise.

Check Out the Academic Departments

When on campus, it is very important to lay eyes on the people that will be teaching the classes that you will be focused on throughout your collegiate experience. The professors and department heads may be able to give you a little insight as to what you can be able to expect from the situation.

Catch a class if possible. Sitting in on a class that is in session will not be too much to ask from a professor. Most will welcome the opportunity.

Be sure to understand that even if you are being recruited to attend a university, these universities are being recruited by you as well. Do not aim to settle on a school for anyone reason. The entire situation can and should work in your favor, or else look elsewhere. The hunt may tire you, but the reward will be special.

CHAPTER FOUR: "WHERE ARE THE SCHOOLS THAT I WANT?"

You could be possibly dealing with a variety of situations as it pertains to your college recruitment right now. You could be a freshman who does not quite have an understanding of what's to come and is trying to do whatever you need to do to put yourself in a position to become a collegiate student-athlete. You could also be a senior, winding up your final year of high school getting ready to bet the house on yourself just for a chance to compete again. No matter who you are, there is no fun in panicking as it pertains to the recruiting process.

The professional opinion that I can give you in regard to this is, to prepare yourself as soon as you can to receive the attention that you want.

That will be the key as it pertains to the ebbs and flows of being recruited. Be sure to be the athlete that has all their eligibility requirements covered, so that if you are not being recruited by a level it is because of **ability and not a lack of preparation.**

Messaging Coaches

Always remember that there are a lot of rules that coaches are required to follow in terms of recruiting and their contracts. Don't over panic if coaches don't reach back all the time or talk to you much at games and events.

As a student-athlete, never have a parent email or direct message on your behalf.

Sample Email/Direct Message

Hello Coach _____,

My name is _____, and I am thoroughly interested in becoming a part of your program. I am part of the class of _____, at _____ high school/college. I am interested in learning more about your program.

I saw that _____ (interesting fact).

This works very well with my ability to _____ (the value you bring to the program).

I compete as a _____ (current sports, positions, and teams).

Here is my highlight tape _____ (link).

Please feel free to contact me or my coaches at

_____

Email for self)

_____

(Phone number for self)

_____

(Email for coach)

_____

(Phone number for coach)

(Add schedule for all sporting events here)

My GPA is _____.

My test scores are _____.

I look forward to meeting with you and learning more about _____ (interesting facts about the school).

Best Regards,

_____

(Printed Name)

Messaging Checklist

- Be sure to include the name, position, and graduating class in the email.

- Send the message from a working professional email or social media page

- Do research to find out who's there (upperclassmen, team accomplishments, and learn the backgrounds of leadership and athletes who are already on campus).

- Always make sure to get your recruiting coach's email.

- Get someone to spell-check all your messages.

- Make a follow-up phone call after your email.

When Contacting Coaches.

Make sure that you make a real introduction with coaches. You can only introduce yourself to someone one time. You can't get a second chance to make an impression, so make it count. Speak clearly, concisely, and look the coach in the eye. Make sure you shake their hand with a firm handshake and be as confident as possible throughout the interaction. Always be sure to introduce all family members who are around you to the couch as well.

Always Answer All of the Coach's Questions Clearly and Truthfully.

Be yourself above all things. Do not play a role in front of a coach, because at some point you'll be exposed. You must demonstrate confidence that comes from being truthful and honest.

When Interacting with Coaches, Never Do These Things!

1. **Never let your parents do all of the talking.** This can't happen because coaches want to know that you as the athlete are truly interested in the school. If your parents are talking more than you, then that gives off the idea that you are not interested in the school.

2. **Never disrespect anyone.** Coaches pay attention to everything you do in the first couple of interactions that they have with you. Don't be the person who bad mouths other athletes, teams, coaches, or schools. This will lead to the coach building a negative representation of who you are. That leads them to potentially ending recruitment, and letting others know how foul of a pe4son that you are. Parents are included in this interaction mistake also. The experiences with coaches should be positive, and they should stay that way. Keep all negatively out of negative reactions.

The game of collegiate athletics is one that rewards the proactive. Have all the answers you can possibly put together before anyone can ask. Students make decisions that impact their ability to play college sports as early as 9th grade. The grades that 9th graders make affect whether they will be able to go to the school of their choice, even if they are athletically dominant enough. The early grades student-athletes receive are just as important as the later grades.

Sometimes even more important than the grades made, the classes taken could also drastically improve a student's probability of receiving early scholarship offers. Classes that are taken by a student-athlete directly influence where they could ultimately end up.

A Story from Coach Juice:

I was a victim of the battle with eligibility, athletics, and the NCAA. I entered high school at a small school in Yermo, California. The classes that I took, I was unaware of, and I passed 9th grade with average grades. Halfway through my 10th-grade year, I transferred to the school I would eventually graduate from in Harker Heights, Texas. I received a lot of college interest because of my on the field performance, but until my senior year, no offers had surfaced. After a long winter, an FCS school that I eventually committed to gave me a call. My recruiting coach had explained to me that getting me eligible was a complex situation. This was the first time a coach broke down to me the issues that colleges ran into me while recruiting me as a student-athlete.

My recruiting coach explained to me that my GPA and SAT sliding scale scores needed some adjustment. In my specific situation, my GPA was too low for the SAT score that I had at the time. He promised me that if I went back and took the SAT, the offer would stand throughout the spring. I took the test and received the score I needed to secure my scholarship. I committed in January during my first visit, shortly before signing day in February.

I went to school in the summer and worked with the team in June and July, without taking any summer courses. All seemed to be falling into place, and then I was met with a tough situation. Two days before the start of fall camp in August, I received a message from my recruiting coach notifying me that I was deemed ineligible by the NCAA due to a course I had taken in 9th grade.

This led to me battling with a bout of depression due to my inability to chase my passion. This story's purpose is to show the importance of meeting the eligibility requirements and checking to make sure that you have done so yourself.

High School Courses Breakdown

D-I Requirements (Most difficult):

Amateur certification and...

- 4 Years of English
- 3 Years of Math
- 2 Years of Natural/Physical Science
- 2 Years of Social Science
- 1 Additional Year of English, Math, or Natural/Physical Science
- Additional Academic Courses (4 years required)
- 10 Core Courses completed prior to starting of 7th semester and 7 of 10 must be a combination of Math, English, or Natural/Physical Science
- Core Course GPA must be 2.3 or above with matching test scores on NCAA Sliding Scale must be eligible to play as a freshman or 2.0- 2.3 to be eligible for a redshirt freshman year.

*Go to fc.ncaa.org to locate the "NCAA Sliding Scale"

D-II Requirements:

Amateur certification and...

- 3 Years of English
- 2 Years of Math (Algebra 1 or higher)
- 2 Years of Natural/Physical Science
- 2 Years of Social Science
- 3 Additional Year of English, Math, or Natural/Physical Science
- Additional Academic Courses (4 years)
- Core Course GPA must be 2.2 or higher with matching test scores on NCAA Sliding Scale to be eligible to play as a freshman.

D-III Requirements:

All Division III schools have their own admissions and eligibility requirements.

The most important piece of the D-III puzzle is being eligible through the eligibility center.

D-III requirements go into depth on the NCAA website.

You always need to make sure that all your core courses are **NCAA-approved.**

NAIA

The NAIA normally requires students to meet academic eligibility requirements for NAIA, graduating high school players must meet 2 of the following 3 criteria as outlined on the NAIA Eligibility website...

1. *Have a total GPA of 2.0 or above on a 4.0 scale*

Score the required composite ACT score (16 if taken prior to April 30, 2019, or an 18 if taken after that date) OR score the required 2-part (Math & Evidence-Based Reading and Writing) SAT Score (860 if taken prior to April 30, 2019, or a 970 if taken after that date)

2. Graduate in the top 50% of their class

The NAIA handbook also states, "All students participating in intercollegiate athletics must be admitted to member institutions under admission standards that are equal to or higher than those applied to the general student body of that institution." One unique aspect about NAIA eligibility is if students meet certain academic requirements at certain points during high school, they may receive eligibility status for NAIA competition before graduating.

Check out some of these helpful resources *in helping gain eligibility…*

Division I Academic Requirements

http://fs.ncaa.org/Docs/eligibility_center/Student_Resources/DI_ReqsFactSheet.pdf

ACT Resource

https://www.act.org/content/act/en/products-and-services/the-act.html

Resources like:

The NCAA Prospect Eligibility center

http://fs.ncaa.org/Docs/eligibility_center/Student_Resources/CBSA.pdf

COLLEGE BOARD SAT PREP RESOURCE

https://satsuite.collegeboard.org/sat

Khan Academy SAT Prep

https://www.khanacademy.org

High School Student Plan Of Action

High School Student-Athlete Plan Of Action

- Apply to schools of interest.
- Send test scores to schools of interest.
- Make periodical admissions office phone calls.
- Reach out to your high school counselor.
- Print the requirements for your schools of interest.
- Get four letters of recommendations

(Action Plan)

CHAPTER FIVE: COLLEGE COMMITMENT

The commitment to any offer that you have received is legally bound by nothing but your word. Once upon a time, a man's (or woman's) verbal commitment would mean everything. In today's world of college athletics, that is not the case in most cases. This ideal is supported by the tornado-like scenarios that are represented due to the "transfer portal", which is where student-athletes go to essentially rechoose the institution that they would like to attend for the next 4-5 years.

The world of athletics has now normalized the flipping of commitments and change in decision-making regarding the potential future of a student-athlete. Sometimes, these scenarios even take place as late as an athlete's senior in high school. Think of this: You have been in communication with a recruiter for three years, and by now you're so invested you have even received your first off-season workout plan from your prospective university. After building these relationships, suddenly changing your decision can be extremely difficult and may even make you feel untrustworthy.

The lower-level school that has occupied most of your interest has continued to keep your attention, but now a higher-level university states that they believe in your abilities and are intending to bestow you a position as a higher-level athlete for their institution. It is extremely important to evaluate this decision in its entirety, no matter how sure you may feel in any situation. Do you turn down the higher-level school out of your vow of loyalty, possibly sacrificing an opportunity that you have been chasing since you began competing in athletics as a young child?

I want whoever is reading this to understand this, life does not afford us many opportunities more than once. Once an opportunity that spikes your interest arises you must choose to answer. Not only do you answer, but you kick the door down with ferocity checking for any remnants of the future that you believe your life has in store for you. If a school comes along and intrigues you, see what could come of the situation. Do your research.

This is not a situation to be likened to cheating on your significant other in a relationship. This is your life. Do not treat your recruitment like a dating season, and in turn allow coaches, friends, or parents the opportunity to cripple you into thinking that you are smaller than your dreams. Some coaches will recoil when you explore other schools, that the decisions that you choose to make for your future have less to do with what everyone else thinks and 100% to do with what in your mind and heart believes is the correct decision moving forward.

I've made a decision, but I think something else might be better...

Please find out what every school has to offer. Please be sure to explore your options, knowing what every school has to offer. Then and only then, any option that you choose to accept, or decline will be your decision-making. The reality for some is that their dream may not be to become an athlete competing at the highest level, some student-athletes truly have aspirations to solely obtain a specified degree that represents the career field they choose to get into post-college. Not only is that great, but that type of understanding and foresight is applauded and encouraged.

Takeaway…

The lone advice that lies in the message is this: Please do not turn down opportunities in collegiate athletics solely for the sake of loyalty. College athletics are not a breeding ground for loyalty. College athletics are a breeding ground for relationships that will be cultivated within the experience and money. Universities (like most major entities) aim to create revenue or money. This is the unfortunate reality that a lot of student-athletes and parents do not truly understand. This is a game that is played for money. This process is driven by money and a lack of this understanding can have you on the fast track to bad decision-making.

When flipping the direction on a decision, please be sure to communicate with all coaches that you have been in contact with the utmost respect. This must be demonstrated even if the respect has not been shown to you. If you ask a college coach what they absolutely cannot stand, they all may say in unison a "big-timer". No college coach wants to be "big timed", most already feel as though they don't make enough money anyway. The last thing a college coach wants is to be "hot-shotted" a 17–18-year-old student-athlete. Make sure you don't burn bridges in your college recruitment.

CHAPTER SIX: FAITH

This chapter is about the faith that it takes. Faith is what you will need when you are faced with distractions. Faith is what you will need as you battle with yourself and the hundreds and thousands of worthy adversaries that will come across your path whether you're ready or not. You will need a tremendous amount of faith to even get out of bed at times. You will get lost on the journey and that is a guarantee. You will be let down at some point, leading you to question the loyalty of people in general. It happens. Do not allow yourself to become a casualty of war. By definition, a casualty is a military person lost through death. This is not an allusion to the idea that you will die throughout the process of recruiting, but rather a warning that without the proper information and guidance anything can happen. You must be well informed and in the right situation to maximize the potential of your opportunities.

Your belief system must always prove its ability to stay rock solid. Being grounded in faith is not only tied to religion, but this concept is also primarily tied to an intense overall belief that things will and can always work out for the better. The faith the size of a mustard seed is all that you need, just like it says in the good book. You will encounter some very dark moments and experiences while you embark on the journey to change your life for the better. Every day at some point you will question the path and wonder whether you will be able to achieve all of the specific goals that you have outlined for your life. Do I want this

THAT bad? This is perfectly normal, and you will need your faith to be battle-tested. Without a rock-solid faith, nothing in this life worth doing is possible for any of us.

The general population of non-athletes perceives the student-athlete life as glamor, fun, and undemanding. I would agree that there are a plethora of amazing moments that transpire during your period of being a student-athlete, but I wouldn't exactly call it a life of leisure. Kristy Carlin, a junior power forward majoring in business management, understands all too well the demands on student-athletes, "Being a student-athlete is challenging because you have to juggle practice schedules and traveling for games with classes," Carlin said. "Most of us have scholarship responsibilities, so we can't afford to fall behind in our schoolwork.". Not only do you have to take care of school and sports obligations, but there are also sacrifices that you have to make to ensure you are at your best athletically. All the fun and freedom that normal college students receive does not apply to the life of a student-athlete.

Time management is one of the most important factors leading to your overall success as a student-athlete. You will be spending plenty of time with a physical therapist for pre-training treatment, having the athletic trainer tape you, warming up for practice, cooling down after practice, traveling back from practices, or seeing the trainers for post-training treatment. Consider team meals, individual meetings with the coaches, or team-organized meetings either, all of which are frequent during the season. Of course, there's also travel time spent on the road. Many full-time students have part-time jobs, but those jobs are usually 20-30 hours a week. A student-athlete spends 40-50 hours a week on their specific sport and other activities relative to the sport. For the most part, that's a full-time job. For college athletes, you must be a full-time student to be eligible to participate in sports, so in essence full-time student with a full-time job.

The recruiting process is a rough one. Have your hard hat ready. Even though this is true, being IN college is much more difficult. Between workouts, practices, study groups, check-ins, the most organized and driven student-athletes have their hands full. Normally individuals turn to groups for support early. Fellowship of Christian Athletes (FCA) is a great option for athletes who identify with Christianity or are without denomination. There are also fraternities, clubs, and other affiliations that student-athletes become a part of to help on their journey of finding their way through their collegiate journey.

The game changes for student-athletes first, because all athletes must realize that they are no longer the man anymore. Although you have been recruited to come onto campus and make a difference, that does not mean that your contribution is to be expected to happen right away. That is key to understanding the level of FAITH that is required to compete in athletics on this level. Everything at this level is about timing. There are many jobs on the line every time you lace up your spikes or pick up the ball. As before stated, you are a commodity first and that usually encompasses long-term plans regarding your future with the program. You mustn't just throw the towel in because things are not going the way that you wanted them to go.

Rodney's Story…

"Rodney was the hometown hero in his town. He was recruited to attend the division institution in his state. As this university was one of the two of its magnitude in his state they had an agenda in regards to Rodney's recruitment. Rodney was recruited by the university for the sole purpose of keeping him from going to the other university within the state. Rodney was under the impression that he was there to make an immediate impact due to the conversations that he had with his recruiting coach at the university.

This was evident during the first couple of months in a school for Rodney as he spent weeks deep within the depth chart of the program's football program. Rodney was not even receiving "garbage time" at the end of games due to the level of success that the team was already enjoying. They had athletes everywhere.

Although Rodney knew this to be the case before he stepped onto campus, the problem lay in the fact that he had not decided to come to college with intentions of being patient. Rodney wanted to play, and he wanted to play now. Rodney started to dabble in risky activity and began to do things that he had never done in the past.

These activities among others ended up spelling demise for the young athlete. He was put behind bars for a charge that he was only associated with because of who he was with during the time. Rodney did not end up getting back on track in collegiate athletics, but he was, fortunately, able to go back to his hometown and make a decent living despite the early adversity that he had faced."

The Bottom Line…

A lack of faith can cost you a lot more than you know. On an athletic level, the best athletes in the respective sports always possess a tremendous amount of faith. This is a requirement if you expect to be a premier student-athlete. The proof is in the statistics. This comes from deep in the inner workings of your soul.

The fire within will light the way! Get around people that care about you and always keep them nearby. These are your accountability partners. These people will never let you struggle for too long. From personal experience, these people usually are in the places where you want to be. The way out of your darkest hour lies within the depths of your spirit and the fibers of your soul. Protect that energy at all costs. Why? Because you will always be worth it.

CHAPTER SEVEN: LEAVING HOME

Now let's get into maybe one of the most controversial topics that you will find in this entire book… leaving home. Why so controversial you ask? Well, sit down and have a seat, there are more than enough reasons going either way why people differ in opinion on this one so much. A high schooler has a lot of ideas going around their heads to go along with the pressure of deciding on what to do post-high school education.

A lot of these ideas are supported by information that may not always be factual. This leaves a large amount of responsibility on the need for student-athletes to keep solid support around, for them to be comfortable in their ability to make smart informed decisions about future endeavors. Some of the significant commonalities of misunderstandings need to be cleared up before taking the next step. Even once a collegiate athlete steps on-campus mental guidance will still be necessary.

Before we lay it on thick in a crash course layout focused on how to thrive and survive throughout this part of the journey, let's take some time out to debunk a few myths.

Myth #1

"I will finally be able to do what I want now, and no one will be able to tell me anything!"

This one is about as false as false gets. Sorry to break it to you, but responsibility for your actions doesn't lead to your 100% freedom quite yet cowgirl. Leaving the nest is an extremely exciting time in a young adult's life. You are finally approaching the legal age for most things, and life may be seeming to finally open up for you. Especially if the plan is to travel hundreds or thousands of miles away to attend school. Anyone with a solid amount of knowledge as it pertains to secondary education would say for your overall development, moving may not be a bad idea. Moving can do a lot for your overall independence development and add a considerable amount of confidence in your ability to make decisions. Although there are some seeds of benefit in this type of situation, decision-making ability does not equate to "freedom to do whatever the heck I want". As a student-athlete, the expectations that most people had for you in high school pale in the face of the amount of prestige and status you will hold at the next level. Even the strictest parents cannot keep the type of watchful eye of that of a community that is interested in where you like to catch a burger with your buddies. **You will be a highly respected role model at the school you attend, you must constantly be thinking about how you are representing the brand of your program in everything you do.** At parties, at a restaurant, at the movies, in the dorms, you name the location and chances are someone could be watching you waiting for you to slip or amaze them with your character. The choice is yours.

The reality is you must be more careful than the regular student body on campus. The pressure to be a student-athlete is not only limited to practices, meetings, workouts, and competitions. The way you are perceived on campus will play a role in your academic, social, and athletic success. So, with this understanding try your best to act as if your mom was watching you every single day of your life, and you will probably be in good shape. I am not saying walk around uptight, and police all of your teammate's fun (besides that is the quickest way to stop getting invites), but rather be in control of your destiny and don't become your worst enemy in your collegiate experience. The hate will be evident and that is inevitable. Some people will be salty because of the position that you are in and there would be nothing they would love to see more than you make a mistake and lose all that you and your teammates have worked hard for so that they will be able to lump you into their student-athlete stereotype graveyard forever. Some people are just miserable, and misery loves company. Don't give a negative person that does not want to see you succeed, fuel to feed their dark evil fire. Come to terms with the reality that everyone may wasn't to see you win and be okay with that. Living in the dorms and waking up to a party at midnight down the hall could seem like a ton of fun at first, but the risk of ruining your reputation on campus should be in your mind playing over and over like a 15 second TikTok.

\

In general, becoming a college student, you will have more freedom (often), than before leaving home. The "catch" is a large amount of want is seen as "freedom" is missing two words that help define the real meaning of freedom in college. These two words are "of" and "choice". Now, let's say it together, **freedom of choice**. This is the most overlooked concept for most college freshmen across the nation. A severe lack of understanding can make you a "one and done" athlete in the collegiate world. These individuals are defined as those who come to campus through the fall and are headed home with a 1.0 GPA, a criminal charge, and an awkward thigh tattoo they don't remember getting. This is a reality for a very high percentage of all collegiate freshmen and incoming freshmen. All freshmen need to understand the risks that could easily become a reality in their lives.

"Know thyself, and know the enemy, fear not 100 battles"
Sun Tzu, The Art of War

Myth #2

Student-Athletes do worse in school than the rest of the student population on campus

This common misconception could not be anything further than the truth. Student-athletes typically do better than most of the student population, even with all the demands that their schedules have. Athletes typically do a lot more since they have less time to work overall. Student-athletes are also afforded additional resources academically to support them as they navigate their busy schedules. The loft expectations are guided with assistance from the academic resources coordinators, position coaches, and head coaches.

Myth #3

Student-Athletes are privileged and can get whatever they want

This is another myth that must be busted for a student-athlete before they join the college ranks. There are people on campus that want to see athletes do well. It is just also important for student-athletes to know that there are also individuals that are on campus who do not want to see you succeed. Entitled spirits are destroyed on the college level. These professors do not know you, and they will fail you. Especially, if you believe that you are a hotshot that doesn't have to do their work. Be conscious of the fact that everyone will not be on your side. Another thing to keep in mind is, the individuals that like you on campus have an idea of who you are, but that may not necessarily be the "real" you. Don't feel the need to keep up an image, because someone else's expectations cannot run your decision-making process. You must do and be the person that makes you happy at all times. Those around you that truly care about you won't judge you. Those that truly care will be understanding and open to the unique presence that you bring to your campus.

CHAPTER EIGHT: COMPETITION

"I want to kill, crush, and outmaneuver everyone. I compete within every moment. But I also want you to win. I just want to beat you by one."-Gary Vaynerchuk

According to Merriam-Webster, the following represents the definition of competition…

Competition:

1: the effort of two or more parties acting independently to secure the business of a third party by offering the most favorable terms.

2: active demand by two or more organisms or some environmental resource in short supply.

Competition is consistently present throughout all of life. Business, relationships, entertainment, academics, and whatever else has a system of measurement and pragmatically through analytics.

There will always be and has always been a **winner and a loser**. If we take it back to the gladiator days, the losers were subject to their lives. This mimics the hierarchy of the food chain as it relates to the animal kingdom, being on top makes you the predator, and all below fall victim as prey.

As this concept relates to becoming and being a student-athlete, **you will always actively compete until you choose that participating in the sport is no longer for you.**

I think the game changed for me when I engaged myself in the mindset that I will not let myself hold the position of my own worst enemy for too long. This is the difference between the good and the great at any mission that an individual embarks on. The mission is to become the best that you can be.

I have been torn between two different ideas regarding competition in my life. There has almost been that "junkyard dog" presence within me for most of my life. Taking the path of becoming a high-level student-athlete requires it. Knowing that you must attack the competition by the throat to secure victory is common knowledge amongst the athletic community. They say that the exhibition of competition bred through the youth sports circuits will show you that. The perspective that many youth athletes adopt could prove to be of their detriment if some level of monitoring is not present in this area.

The key question that is usually the guiding factor is: *"When are you competing with others too much?"*

Good Competition

The defining quality of good competition is where there is an opportunity for growth as a result of the competitive spirit and participation. The competition is taking something out of the athlete that wouldn't come out without a challenge. The challenge is what pushes an individual to their limit because of the goal of defeating another competitor. Scientifically, it is proven that physical activity versus another person brings out the best within us. Once we reach the limit, we push past it to keep up if we are behind. Another possibility is that we reached our limit, and then we pushed forward harder to remain ahead or widen the gap. Either way, the presence of someone else helps us keep pushing.

Robbie and Janey's story:

Robbie and Janey were the best tennis players on their high school team. The level they played at was built throughout the continuous practice sessions that they participated in outside of school. The two always played on the same teams from 5th grade until their senior years in high school. They were both ranked 5th and 1st in the state respectfully. Although they practice relentlessly against one another in practice, they were the best of friends. Robbie and Janey were almost inseparable. When asked why they were so close each would give the same answer. "Iron sharpens iron, as one man sharpens another". Robbie and Janey felt **disrespected** when another player would step up against them in a practice set. These two young ladies were obsessed with getting better and love the fact that they had the opportunity to go against one of the best in the state daily. Their fearlessness of competition proceeded their dominance on the court.

Bad Competition

Bad competition can be defined as an athlete competing to the point where competition is too focused on what another person is doing and losing sight of the most important opponent, self. The fixation on another individual is not good for the mental state of an athlete. You can never be more focused on what is going on outside of you, than what is happening inside of you. **Comparison is the thief of joy.** You will never be happy doing what you do, while constantly keeping an eye out for the competition. The competition is only there to pull out what is already inside of **YOU**. The competition should serve as more of a motivating source, instead of self-defeating entertainment. When you are constantly feeling anxiety, fear, excessive nervousness, helplessness, and lack confidence as it relates to the competition it is usually due to a disconnection from self. We have to always remember that the competition does not control the outcome of the competition, **WE DO.**

Sun Tzu in "The Art Of War" has a great quote about effective competition:

"The victorious strategist only seeks battle after the victory has been won, whereas he who is destined to defeat first fights then afterward looks for victory."

The separation lies in the preparation. Proper preparation keeps away a bad competitive spirit because then a woman understands that the only person that she is really up against is herself.

Were you disciplined enough to wake up and make it to all of your workouts this week?

Did you make goals that you completed daily?

Did you get at least one percent better today?

Are you giving amazing effort and showing a great attitude, in the classroom, on the field, and in the community?

These are all questions one must ask themselves if competition is proving to become a problem in their life. **Competition can be stressful if you do not prepare for it correctly**

PART II: CAN YOU TRULY B.E.L.I.E.V.E?

The foundation of this book is now laid down as a framework that provides you with some of the basic survival skills you will need on your journey. This information will lead you on the trail to becoming the best student-athlete that you can possibly be. Don't let the future be something that shows up in your life by happenstance or accident. The way to be sure that this cannot happen is through a deliberate plan that includes a variety of action steps.

At this time, the book will be broken down into the fundamental important steps to using the college recruiting and playing experience to your ultimate benefit. The x-factor to this book lies within a very specific strategy that can be understood by the acronym B.E.L.I.E.V.E. To truly B.E.L.I.E.V.E you must **build**, **educate**, **love**, **increase**, **energize**, **visualize**, & then **execute**.

When all skills are practiced effectively and with repeated and consistent effort... the life that collegiate athletics will afford you and your family for many years to come. Through extensive research, the study of hundreds of athletes, and personal experiences, this method has been developed to maximize the potential of the student-athlete AFTER the game is over.

Take out the notebook or open your notes on your phone so you can be able to fully absorb the information that you are about to read. Revisit the information over and over to really be able to change the direction and your life forever.

Now, let's start **BELIEVING!**

CHAPTER ONE: BUILD YOUR FOUNDATION

The foundation of a building is the most important part of the structure itself. It allows the elements to be able to age the framework but still leaves the overall building standing tall. In this stage, you should be in a serious building frenzy. Stacking skill sets on top of each other at a very high rate. Build your faith in yourself. Prepare for your future with intense enthusiasm knowing that everything you do today, could change your life tomorrow.

You only must be in the right place, at the right time, building your foundation for things to go right in a marvelous way. There are two sides to every sword so it is important to know that this same concept could end up working the other way around as well. The inability to build a solid foundation could spell doom later down the road to success.

Bad crowds, drugs, excessive partying, unhealthy relationships, unhealthy diets, all can end up sending you down the student-athlete dungeon if you are not careful. The build is important to the potential of your career. Don't know where to start? Start where you want.

Here's a great place to start:

1. What is the biggest dream that you have in your life?'

---

2. Who on this planet is doing things and living a lifestyle you want to live, and is willing to share information with you about how they can live as they do?

_____

Imagine taking a course that is challenging for most students. Now imagine missing at least a day's worth of lectures every other week during the regular season. Not only are you behind the rest of the class, but you are on the road. You must teach yourself the missed material from the back of a bumpy bus, an airplane, or in the computer room of a hotel. There's no professor or teaching assistants present, to ask questions, or review a difficult chapter; there's just you and the textbook. What if you need to stay up late and finish an assignment, but you have an important game the following day. What do you do? What do you sacrifice? How do you manage your time?

The answer is that, if you are not 100% on top of every one of your assignments and if you are not in constant contact with your professors you will not succeed. If you are not willing to do what regular students do, but in harsher environments, you will not succeed.

Not maintaining a 2.0 could cost you your eligibility, scholarship, and possibly get you kicked out of school. This is the risk you take when agreeing to become an athlete in college.

My mother, my greatest mentor, has a saying she has always told me: "Lack of prior planning, leads to piss poor performance". This quote idolizes the concept that I hope you absorb from this section of the BELIEVE strategy.

Your life once you begin to embark on your journey becomes a movie. You play the role of the main character and the casting director. Contact coaches every day, post highlights everywhere, go to as many camps as possible, take your ACT/SAT, do all the things that sound like they may have something to do with where you are going. Link up with a strong mentor to help guide you down the path that you want to go.

CHAPTER TWO: EDUCATION OF SELF

The more you know the more you grow. Learn everything that there is to learn about the process. This is a crucial part of your development toward your goal. Ignorance is the reason most people fail at anything so DO YOUR RESEARCH. Don't go into a situation without knowing everything there is to know about the new situation.

This book is being written in the information age. Today's day in age is tailored to the individual that is dedicated to learning what is going to be prevalent to what they need to know today.

In order to maximize your ability in the step you must follow two steps in a cyclical pattern that goes as follows:

- Learn what to do
- Apply what you have learned

It is as simple as that. Don't complicate the learning process. Learn what you need to know about the upcoming situation in the depth that will be most beneficial for your journey. Once you have learned all of the information that you need, it is time to go to work using the newfound information that you have gained. Information is useless until it is applied. The application of knowledge in the form of execution is king.

As it pertains to secondary education, there are many things to educate yourself on, starting with funding. If you are not going to be in a situation where your school is being paid for (and even if you are), do some research on grants and scholarships that could be available for you to be able to take advantage of. If you are a minority, there are many grants and scholarships out there for you. The only deciding factor on who will receive the extra money to go to school is, who are the students that will do the homework and apply for the limited opportunities to be awarded this money-making school more affordable.

Most school counselors have a pretty good base-level knowledge of how to begin seeking out grants and scholarships, so be sure to use them as a resource. The next best resource in the area would be the academic advisors located at the college that you want to be at. They are interested in having you attend the school, and after seeing that you have an interest in being a student most advisors will go above and beyond to get you set up with the correct financial support to get you into school at a price point that works for you and your family.

Find the schools you are interested in and begin to learn about the great things and commonly known bad things about the school.

What you know is your greatest wealth, but what you don't know is your greatest risk.

In regard to when you are actually on campus, there is one place that ALL freshmen need to start in their crash course of how to survive the education step of the B.E.L.I.E.V.E method. That is **GO TO CLASS**. I know, I know it's simple, and it should go without saying right? If you are reading this book and you have already attended college then you understand how uncommon this step is for a lot of college freshmen. Let's be honest. College life for a freshman on campus is very distracting for most 18–19-year-olds that are just now getting some of their first tastes of freedom. Some of these students frankly just don't know what to do. They show up to campus and don't have any books, or they cannot locate some of their classes for the first two months, or maybe the workload in these classes could be proving to be too much for the student-athlete to juggle as it works together with classes and meetings.

The veteran student-athlete needs to stay on top of education as well. Always understand that you are supposed to be in school to gain a new understanding from the information that you are receiving while you are participating in your classes. These classes are preparatory for your career readiness, so you must take heed to the strength of the information that these professors are releasing to you in the form of lectures.

A major set of skills that can help benefit you in this domain can be broken down into four different major pillars. The major pillars that I would use to help with your comprehension of any skills that you wish to acquire in life or school.

Listen to what you want to learn about as much as possible (lectures, YouTube, social media, Discussions with peers and experts)

Read all information that resembles the information that you are wanting to learn. Know how the terms are spelled and how they connect to each other. Find out the terms about the topic that create confusion for you and do research on those specific words. Become an expert in the terminology of the subject that you are wanting to learn about.

Speak to anybody willing to listen to you talk about the topic that you are wanting to learn. This is a very important process in the self-education process because this will start to make the information your own. You will be able to start to paraphrase (put in your own words) information that you are still turning over in your mind. During this step in your education process, you can go to the learning "gym" ad strengthen your linguistic ability which supports your metacognition. Metacognition is defined as the process of thinking about "how" you think.

Writing: Always write down everything that you hear about the information that you are hoping to learn. You should write all the time because it will allow you the opportunity to transport information from real-time into future time, to assist you in the application process of your overall learning experience.

Takeaway:

This step is for the student-athletes who are aiming to take their career to the next level no matter where they are currently. The student-athlete rolling into their graduate senior season or the junior in high school filtering through letters hoping for that first offer. All students will need to load up on education. Athletes must always be expected to be students first. In most situations, people expect athletes to not be as driven, organized, and passionate in the classroom setting. DO NOT BE THIS ATHLETE AT ALL COSTS. The B.E.L.I.E.V.E strategy is only for student-athletes who are aiming to change the lives of themselves and their families through the college athlete lifestyle that is so heavily revolved around sports. Even if you ask the most decorated athletes of all time, you will find most detailing that the value from the collegiate experience lies in the relationships and the education.

As an athlete, it is also important to add to your athletic skill set through your skill study. The easiest way to study skills is by a simple YouTube search of highlights and full games of different college and professional players and teams. This will allow you to educate yourself on the way the game is "normally" played. You will be able to build and add to your skillset using the abilities of others that you closely observe.

The internet can serve as another coach for you when it comes to taking your play to the next level. Always make sure anything that you wish to apply to your performance matches up with what your coaches are asking of you every single day. The combination of information from your coaching staff and self-research will put you miles ahead of the competition after long.

Teaching yourself

Imagine taking a course that is challenging for most students. Now imagine missing at least a day's worth of lectures every other week during the regular season. Not only are you behind the rest of the class, but you are on the road. You must teach yourself the missed material from the back of a bumpy bus, an airplane, or in the computer room of a hotel. There's no professor or teaching assistants present to ask questions or review a difficult chapter; there's just you and the textbook. What if you need to stay up late and finish an assignment, but you have an important game the following day.

What do you do? What do you sacrifice? How do you manage your time? The answer is that if you are not 100% on top of every one of your assignments if you are not in constant contact with your professors if you are not willing to do what regular students do but in harsher environments, you will not succeed2. Not maintaining a 2.0 could cost you your eligibility, scholarship and possibly get you kicked out of school. This is the risk you take when agreeing to become an athlete in college.

CHAPTER THREE: LOVE

The next step in the fundamental pillars of the B.E.L.I.E.V.E strategy is good old-fashioned love. The kind of love that does not notice anything but hope, faith, and passion. The type of love that is as deep and as vast as any large body of water on this planet. This is so critical for multiple reasons. These reasons are not as warm and fuzzy as the traditional views we have of love.

These qualities are strengthened through the darkness, depression, anxiety, and self-defeating thoughts we often experience. You will run into A LOT of disappointment throughout the process of getting into your school and living out your dream of being a successful student-athlete. You will need to be in love with the process entirely. The process will test your love for what you are doing time and time again. You will have to be sure to keep your mind where it needs to be through some very deep soul searching. There are a few questions that, when revisited frequently enough, will keep your eyes on the prize and your feet on the ground.

"Do I really want to go to the next level?"

This question is strategically listed first for a reason. Here goes a few things that you must understand:

- **You will have more meetings and practice than you will have a personal life.**
-
- **You will not be at home every weekend and be a successful student-athlete**
-
- **Money will become an issue at some point.**
-
- **You cannot just show up to class and pass.**
-
- **Your coaches are now taking on the roles of your parents.**

There is a lot more than just that could be eligible to be added to the list of reasons why you must be mentally prepared for the challenge you will be faced with. These challenges are not meant to deter you from the journey, but rather to excite you. After all, all great athletes love a good challenge. It is very important to make sure you are wanting to go to the next level because it is something you want to do, nonetheless.

Jordan's Fading Passion.

"Jordan was the top volleyball player at her school, as well as one of the best in the state. She was heavily recruited by many schools at the start of the recruiting process during her sophomore and junior years in high school, but due to poor grades and character issues, most schools did not make it much further than a phone call with her head coach. Jordan had little to no motivation to go to the next level to play volleyball and did the bare minimum to stay eligible year after year.

She told her coaches at times that she would be happy just getting a job at the local boutique that her aunt owned when she graduated.

Although Jordan's drive to play at the next level was completely absent, her amazing level of talent kept college coaches writing and calling her cell phone. As her senior season came to an end, a very prestigious university reached out to Jordan and her mother informing them that she would need to take a few classes in the summer, then retake the ACT exam she'd taken the year before and they could guide her into being accepted at the institution.

Jordan was excited! Jordan worked extremely hard to get her grades up, completed the exam again, and got the score that she needed, then she enrolled into the university in the fall.

Shortly after the first six months on campus, Jordan realized something. She'd never really wanted to be in college in the first place. Her passion was clothing and she longed to work with her aunt's marketing team for the boutique she was running. Jordan withdrew from school before the start of her second semester realizing that aloof the practices, meetings, and schoolwork was never really what she longed for in the first place."

There are hundreds of Jordan's all over the nation taking opportunities to go to the next level...just to take them. These individuals had no intentions of being in college and believed that this is what they wanted due to the pressure that they have received or because they were following the crowds, they identified themselves with in high school. There are a lot of situations where parents that mean well pressure their children to go to college even though the reality is that was never a goal for their child in the first place. This is the first question that needs to be analyzed in full if you want to take the leap of faith and change the trajectory of your family's lives through your education and the sport that you love.

This awesome opportunity can be drudgery and almost slave work if it is not something that you truly want for your life. The commitment that it will take requires a dedication to the process, unlike anything else. The demands on your time will be constant, your body will be consistently sore, your mind will doubt itself, but your love for the game will pull you through.

What are you willing to give up while becoming successful?

This question is the most thought-provoking of the two. This question has multiple dimensions to it, and it should not be able to be answered easily. If you can answer this easily, then that probably means you did not give much thought to it. The process of becoming, then being a student-athlete is one of many peaks and valleys. This process will present situations that will be completely out of the student athlete's control. These are not the things to pay attention to. The things that can be controlled include:

- The amount of sleep you receive.

- What you eat.

- How you manage time.

- How disciplined you are.

- Your overall work ethic.

True love for something is directly correlated to the amount that you are willing to sacrifice for that specific person, place, or thing. This level of sacrifice will look different for us all. The main thing is, if you love something then you are more inclined to protect it. Protect the opportunity to come or the one that has already presented itself. Protect the love that you have for your future and the futures of those who depend on you. Protect the reputation that you have built and all the things that you represent.

Be sure to root yourself in love and compassion that is the root of the B.E.L.I.E.V.E strategy. This makes all the struggles worth it. Don't forget that is the essence of what this is all about. Along the journey, a lot of people will try to test your loyalty to the game. They will try to entice you along the way, but you must stand firm in the face of temptation. Not to say this will be easy, but it will be worth it. Working on your academics and your chosen sport with a spirit of love will drive you to insane heights that you never knew you were able to reach.

Thoughts on connecting with your love and compassion....

What moves your spirit around like nothing else that you have ever known? What thing could make you the most uncomfortable if there's nothing done to fix it?

Who are the people in your life that you do not want to let down? Who do you see every day when you wake in the morning and have to be at workouts promptly at 5:30 am?

Write these people down in a journal. Look over these names every day and understand that these people and the reasons that you cannot let them down will form your "Why".

Your "why" can also be defined as your anchor to your goals. The waves guide your ship to its destination. You will struggle more than you need to if you cannot effectively identify what your "why" is and how that moves your spirit to achieve the great things that the creator has in store for your life.

CHAPTER FOUR: INCREASE EVERYTHING

Welcome to the component that you may not have the most fun with, but proper implementation will lead to you looking like an overnight success to the novice observer. This will turn the good to great, the ordinary to extraordinary, and the better than most to the best available. Simply put, this is the level where you make sure you do everything that you can do.

Then, you do it repeatedly to cement it in your psyche as a habit. This does not require a complex or dynamic level of understanding to master this concept. This requires a driven person on a mission, with an insatiable desire to conquer and take more of a mental and physical beating than ever before.

Think Texas. Do everything you've done before, just make it a point to do it BIGGER and BETTER. Leaders lead from the front, and this is done through the work.

Some of you may be thinking, "More? I am already doing so much!". To this, I say yes, this could be a true statement. To those of you that feel as though you are already doing a lot now, and it would be an incredible miracle to pull off being more productive than you are at this moment, I have a few questions.

Question #1:

How are you measuring your workload, and what is this amount being compared to?

Let's face it. We are people and we always believe that the world revolves around us, naturally. It can be difficult to step outside of yourself and truly see the way your productivity looks from a 3rd-person point of view. You may be working and executing at a high rate, but someone is always doing better, working longer, and going through more pain and sacrifice to achieve their destination. This understanding is critical to truly creating an increase in what you are doing daily. Therefore, constant competition, and building a competitive edge are important. This is because as we compete, we lose focus on what we brought into the competitive situation with, and the chief aim of coming out of this opportunity is victorious.

The increase is naturally built into the spirit of competition. If you can help it, don't always train alone. Bring a teammate or someone that is wanting to get into shape. The spirit of shared struggle and working to build strength will push you to a level of productivity that will challenge you. The biggest way that this challenges you is through the stretching of your work capacity.

Work capacity is the ability of an individual to work until exhaustion forcing them to take a break and return at a later time or date.

The build of an individual's ability to work can show rapid growth from constant competition and maintenance of work capacity.

This is not just physical, but also psychological or mental. The mind also holds within it a capacity for work so once it stretches itself to exhaustion, at the end of that experience you can expect to be at least one percent better. Imagine this. What if you grew at least 1% every single day for a year or 365 days? At the end of that year, you would be at least 365% better than you are right now!

This is not considering that some days you may even grow in certain areas by 5%, 10%, or 15%. The idea is to just keep growing. Growth is king in the increasing principle of the B.E.L.I.E.VE. strategy.

If you want to take things to the next level, your measuring stick must ALWAYS be adjusted. Good yesterdays, turn into bad tomorrows. You are always getting better or getting worse. Find a mentor, or an accountability partner to push you. The fundamental purpose of any endeavor is to be better than you were yesterday.

Question #2:

If your wildest dreams were to happen today, do you have the systems, disciplines, and life structures to maintain them?

Okay, so before you say you are ready to be the all-American MVP with a 4.0 GPA, or you're ready to land the person you dream about…think about this. At this point, everything that you have ever done has prepared you for what you have RIGHT NOW. That's it. The unseen will always remain the unseen and new levels present new devils. The separation for you will lie in your preparation. Your talent can ABSOLUTELY be ahead of what you may be truly ready for, let that sink in.

Imagine, you step onto campus the best player on the team, and you have the organizational skills of a 4th-grade student. You will let your team down when it matters.

Maybe you've been an "a little above average" athlete for the bulk of your athletic career and in the biggest moment, you are called to be in a leadership position. The point is this: the opportunity is coming, but will you be ready when it comes?

CHAPTER FIVE: ENERGIZE YOURSELF!

You've decided to build your foundation, you are seeking out the education to take your game to the next level, you're falling in love with the process, & you've increased everything you can possibly think of. Now it's time to find that juice. That thing that makes you a next-level competitor. The reason why the opposition always must account for you. The engine drives your ability to bring it every time you lace up.

This chapter does not refer to caffeinated drinks, pills, or manufactured energy sources. Sustainable energy can only be infused through proper diet and nutrition.

Let's get scientific first.

The two things you need to understand are the leaders for creating and maintaining the functioning of energy in our bodies: one being the mitochondria "the powerhouse" of our cells, and the ATP (adenosine triphosphate) a.k.a "the energy currency of our cells.

This is not a science book nor am I a leader in the study of biology, but as an athlete, the understanding of your body is **VITAL** to achieving record-breaking, game-changing performances all while maintaining healthy relationships and practicing self-love. The mitochondria store ATP, which powers most of the body's metabolic process. In other words, this is the process in which the body burns food to turn it into energy.

This process is helpful in the explanation of why a budding student-athlete superstar, or an everyday person just wanting the best for themselves, should take diet very seriously.

Natural Energy Solutions

Some ways that you can naturally keep your vessel energized and ready to attack your goals include:

1. Control your stress
2. Lighten your load
3. Exercise more
4. Avoid Smoking
5. Restrict your sleep
6. Eat for energy
7. Use caffeine to your advantage
8. Limit Alcohol
9. Drink water

As a general statement:

Diet is a major contributor to energy for an athlete. The elite student-athletes have this area covered. Do not run the risk of being sluggish in the 9th inning, the fourth quarter, or the last set.

Here is a link to an awesome food pyramid to help guide your daily dieting: **https://www.military.com/military-fitness/nutrition/food-pyramid**

CHAPTER SIX: VISUALIZATION

Visualization is seeing what you are about to do before you go to complete the action. This is the act of making sure you complete a mental image in the most vivid fashion that truly serves as a display for what you want to really happen.

Imagine this:

You are a varsity football player, a leader of the unit talking to yourself supercharging your belief system mentally through positive affirmations. "I can do this", "I know I can do this", " I've been working all year for this moment". You are on the field. You are standing at the forty-yard line of a football field. You are looking down into the endzone on a Friday evening. You look at the scoreboard and it is the third quarter. The scoreboard indicates that there are four minutes left to go for the period. It says that it is fourth down, and you can literally feel the tension. It is 4th down with one yard to go for the opposition.

You are currently on defense. You are the linebacker standing in the middle of a crowded line of scrimmage, you know that if you take any steps backward then the offense may gain a conversion by way of taking the one-yard that they still need to stay on the field. You creep forward and you begin to feel your palms start to sweat. Now, your chest begins to beat as it has only when you've felt the most important moments arise in your life.

"Boom", "Boom", "Boom".

You hear the crowd roar and the band's music is starting to pick up.

Suddenly, you no longer can hear a sound. You are ready to go. The competitive juices are starting to flow to every limb and extremity in your body. You start to feel the adrenaline rushing throughout the body, so you let out a yell from the core of your stomach.

The quarterback starts his cadence.

"Blue 42!" "Blue 42" "Set, Hit!"

You take a quick-twitch step straight into the wall of players standing directly in front of you. You meet the ball carrier at the point of contact. Without hesitation or misstep, you wrap your arms around his body, running your feet as fast as you can tolerate. His body feels light. As you both hit the ground, you realize what just happened. You've just made the play that stopped his forward momentum, helping your team be successful at the goal for this play. Your teammates yell and cheer you on off the field as the crowd applause feels you with excitement.

Scenario #2

It is the last track meet of the year. You line up and you shake your legs out. You can feel your calves feeling as limber as they have ever felt all season. You hear the last words that your coach spoke to you before you stepped foot on the track.

"Be quick and smooth"

You align your blocks. You are being extra careful to be sure that you have the proper distance from the starting line and your first block. Now, you check that you have the proper distance from the starting line to your second block. Now, you take the time to walk back into them both very slowly. You take a deep breath in, then you exhale. You catch the scent of the popcorn from a nearby fan. You know what on the command from the gun starter to step into your blocks. Your heart is beating so loudly, that you just are hoping to still be able to hear the gun.

"Runners take your marks"

"Get set!"

Your fingers are pressing to the white of the starting line. You feel your rear raise and now the tension in your left calf starts to build.

"POW!"

You shoot out from the start staying low and controlled. Now you feel like you are on a plane. It feels as if you are just gliding across the track. Now, you're smoothly transitioning into each phase of your race.

What we have just done is experience a detailed visualization process that successful student-athletes produce for themselves prior to competitions or approaching situations where there is a clear desired outcome. To become consistently successful, it is important to be able to SEE your situation as a success, as though it already has come to fruition. Visualization is a major benefactor in why people can constantly reproduce success. It is easier to reproduce success when you know how it looks. When you have gone through multiple situations and outcomes it aids in the development of your confidence and your self-esteem as it pertains to the task at hand. Visualization practices are beneficial if done once in the morning, then again while practicing or working out.

It is important to practice visualization while you work out because as you begin to see the "big picture" and gain a better understanding of why you are doing what you are doing, you will become more motivated to move towards your goal with the best mindset needed to create your success. You will need to have a clear mindset and understanding of the ups and downs of the competition or the situation that you are currently in. Seeing your goal clearly will help you better attain your goal.

Visualization can also be practiced with a vision board. A vision board maps out what you plan to do, when you plan to do it, and what you need to do to complete those plans. Great people create plans and execute those plans. Great athletes, great scientists, greatest teachers, great nurses, great entrepreneurs, all VISUALIZE the success, failures, and sacrifices tied to the goal that they want.

Visualization is key. When you visualize, always see yourself as your best and highest self. See yourself as the result of your training. See yourself as the result of your mental preparation. See yourself as a result of the hours and hours of hard work that you are about to put in.

DO NOT SEE YOURSELF AS YOU ARE RIGHT NOW.

See yourself as you will be IN THAT MOMENT, because of the work that you are putting in right now. The visualization component of the B.E.L.I.E.V.E method is very important because it allows you to step into the most powerful self that you can become. You will not become anything that you cannot see (without a shadow of a doubt) for yourself. If you can see success, then you will be successful. Everything that I can see, I will be. Once it can be truly seen, then now it becomes a part of the internal belief system.

Then, finally, once it is believed whole-heartedly it is now time to work with the universe as partners in achieving your wildest dreams become a reality. You will never be stopped once this concept and consistent practice has become a ritual and routine for you. Never seeing yourself as a loser, failure, or slouch will pay off. See yourself as the most solution-based person that you can see yourself becoming.

Greatness leaves clues

Keep watching greatness. Anyone and anything great in your field you should study to no end. In your visualization practices, you allow yourself to be able to pattern yourself using the great examples that you have studied. As a ballet dancer, you can study the greatest ballet dancers of all time and you can form your style around the type of ballerina you need to be to sit at the top in your field. Now, you will be able to pick up physically what you need by doing it first mentally. This will make things a lot easier through the process of using visualization as a supplemental workout to what you do every single day.

Visualization gives people more reps to get better, as well as practice without physical fatigue. Therefore, most coaches will tell athletes to be sure to get mental reps. When athletes get mental reps, they time their reps by two or three. Now that you are paying attention you get more information, and as you get more information you apply it to your mental image of yourself in the situation. This makes it less difficult to implement the new skills and moves that you learn. Paying attention to greatness gives you more information and the application of that information to yourself in the situation makes new skills and moves learned along with the nuances of your athletic position more practical for you.

Once it is your turn to step into your physical repetition, you have already done these things mentally that will make you a better athlete. Great teammates, great athletes, great coaches, can make the first time you've done something the 5th time you've done something, maximizing your reps tremendously.

Visuals are king **because what you can see will always determine what you can be.**

CHAPTER SEVEN: EXECUTE

Execution is made up of a lot of macro and micro-decisions. The macro is the larger driving force that influences your behavior. This includes your dreams and goals. These macro decisions met with "follow-through" led to tremendous results. If you have an overall want to help your TEAM win a national or state championship, you are thinking in the macro realm. The macro thought pattern and internal drive, motivate its micro partners in the execution process. As you progress through the life of a student-athlete you will learn that the bigger your goals are, the more accountable you will need to be to reach your expectations of success. The way to successfully stay in the macro is tied to your discipline and determination to become who you want to be and how bad you want to go where you say you want to go.

Think of the macro action steps as the generals in the field of battle. These actions primarily serve to guide most of your daily actions. Like the macro processes, the micro-instruments in the execution model. These are the very few steps located within our days that end up making a BIG difference. These things break down to every minute of your day. Including the time that you wake up in the morning, the way that you speak with family and friends, and even the types of social media you choose to engage in. The micro-systems are important to help you understand the "Big Picture".

Think about this, when you see a picture up close you may have a hard time figuring out what it is. You would need to back away for a distance to see what is happening. Your daily habits are developing a picture of who you will become each day. Although you may not be able to see the picture every day, it is important to be able to trust that the correct moves on the micro-level will create your macro reality in the future ("Big Picture")

LOYALTY VS. DISHONOR

The very small decisions like deciding on dinner on a Monday evening after a long day of practice and school, or whether you should head home for the weekend knowing you have a mid-term paper next week separate the "good" from the "best to ever do it".

This is where the rubber meets the road on a racetrack, and the best part is that being loyal to your success process is not based on your ability level. Any person in this world can reach the top of their mountain through a consistent level of dedication, confidence that doesn't recognize failure, and an insanely incredible amount of effort.

The commitment to making these little decisions happen regardless of **circumstances** or **feelings** is most important. This proves the principle of loyalty and proof will be soon to visit in the future. A lack of loyalty to the small details required for your goals is dishonorable. It is dishonor and disgraceful to say there are things that you want from your life that you are willing to do the grunt work to receive. Don't ask for gifts in this life, if doing the small things correctly is not a priority for you. You have to love the process of success and in turn, you must show your love through the cultivation of your **priorities** and **values**.

How Can We Align Our Priorities and Our Values With Our Goals?

The things that you see as **priorities** are the things that you see as most important, so they end up at the top of your to-do list. Execution is all about completing things, and completion is the close cousin to **focus**. The reality of life in school, sports, jobs, churches, politics is that even though little things added up equal a successful "Big Picture", everything is not important enough to spend valuable focus time on it. Therefore, a priority list for one day should max out in between **three to four tasks**.

The rest of the things on your schedule are things that need to get done, but they may not be as important today.

A great priority list needs to include things that you have written down for your entire day.

Example:

Tuesday's Priority List

- Complete grocery shopping

- Meet with my position coach for film

- Go to the library for two hours

A priority list can help you take immediate action leading you closer to your goals, every day. All sustained great things come from a plan. Beware of the things you let happen first in your life, you have less time than you think.

Priority Story:

Leo is a skilled lumberjack that does an excellent job and has 10 years of quality experience as a lumberjack. Leo's ability to do what he does has made him and his family all the money that they own. A recent opportunity has presented itself to Leo for him to become a welder within a family business that his uncle owns. The opportunity will pay Leo more money, but it will require a year of training for a new position. Leo's true calling is being a lumberjack. In this situation, Leo has a good problem with getting to be able to decide between quality opportunities. The current opportunity is what Leo has wanted all his life, why in the world would he leave? What if Leo had a baby after already having four kids who are eating their weight in money. The money in this situation would prove to appeal to him more at the time causing a shift in his priority list from peace, to more pay."

The list of priorities that we create runs our daily lives and they **clearly define what we are going to say "no" to.**

As a top-tier student-athlete, you must be comfortable saying "no" to a lot of things if you aim to secure the visions, aspirations, and dreams that you say you truly want. **Beware of excessive partying, fast food, alcoholic beverages, late nights, and drug use. Consistent overuse in these areas is the leading cause for self-sabotage in student-athletes!**

All of these actions play an important role in the decline of athletic and academic performance, which is a student athlete's main priority. Saying "no" to things gives strength to your ability to execute. Where focus flows, your energy goes. The less cluttered that your life is, the more focused on making your dreams a reality you will be.

Your **values** are those things in your life that you live by and make up the core of who you are.

Values are what you believe in, what you live for, how you see people, how you see success and failures, and most importantly how you see yourself. When you are clear about the things you say that you want the actions attached to those things you just do.

The goal is to create habits that you can stack on top of each other telling the universe that you are not going to be denied. Then through consistent relentless actions, the things that were once difficult for you yesterday will become just another task that you normally execute tomorrow.

Do your values align with the things that you say you want from your life? If yes, what more can we do to take things to the next level? If not, what things can we do to align our actions **TODAY!**

Wherever you are, get loyal and marry your process, then once you have decided to get to work **now**.

CHAPTER EIGHT: REST AND RECOVERY

"When you rest, you catch your breath and it holds you up, like water wings…"
— Anne Lamott

"There is virtue in work and there is virtue in rest. Use both and overlook neither." — Alan Cohen

This is one of the most important concepts that will be expanded on within this book. The idea behind rest and recovery for a student-athlete, and its overall importance in their development. Most people don't understand the value of taking a break and resting when it is needed. Grind culture is real, and there is nothing easy about juggling a school workload while making sure your body can perform to the level that you want it to. The key to balance is rest and even more specifically sleep. This balance can be achieved through rest and recovery, which will keep all your physical weapons razor-sharp, while a lack of rest will make those same weapons dull and ineffective. Sleep will make you more alert and aware of the targets that you are aiming to crush.

The brain fog created by drowsiness can take down the most elite athlete. Most individuals who argue with this idea rarely can support their stance with scientific data. They normally say things like "I never sleep and look how much I can do!". This is the mindset of an athlete content with where they are. The mindset of an individual unwilling to sacrifice who they are currently, for who they will become.

Student-Athletes must schedule in leisure time. If you like scrolling social media or playing video games, put it in your schedule! All student-athletes must schedule a way to release themselves of their daily tensions, and a great job of balancing will make you more effective overall.

There are multiple ways that an individual can promote proper rest within their busy lifestyle. Let's take some time to discuss a few...

Make yourself a schedule

Create a schedule that makes sure that you get your schoolwork priority tasks done first. This will provide the opportunity for you to really fit in the rest that you need. You could try your best to schedule most of your day's events like your classes, your work schedule, practices, **in the morning** or **the evening**. This strategy will allow you to create more free time; leading to you being able to create time for **rest**. The most important part of this equation is consistency.

JD's Story:

JD had a problem with being on time. JD was the best athlete on her track team as a sophomore at a Division II University located in Florida. She won conference track and field championships in three different events during her freshman year. She competed in the 100-meter, 200 meters, and 400-meter sprint races. She currently holds the school record in the 200 meters, through a year and a half of athletic competition. Although JD experienced what seemed like pre-destined success on the track, she was in love with a lifestyle choice that ultimately became her demise. JD was in love with late-night parties, smoking sessions, and candy binges.

These would keep her up until **2 am and 3'oclock am regularly** on school nights. JD started school with these habits and saw early success, so she didn't see these "vices" as an issue. She worked very hard and did all the things that she was asked to do as a student-athlete. The barrier showed up during the summer of her sophomore year during a cold day of winter training for the upcoming indoor track season.

JD was finishing up repeat 200-meter sprints when she felt a "pop" behind her leg nearing the end of a team workout. She was diagnosed by the team doctor with a strained hamstring that required 3-4 weeks of rest. JD's habits continued to leave out rest at night, and JD struggled to heal over the time that was recommended for the level of injury that she had. JD's coaches and teammates were confused as to why she was never able to return to the level of performance that she had shown the year before. JD didn't understand that **rest is key to recovery from injury.** Unfortunately, a lack of sleep, poor time management, and lackluster diet ended up leaving JD as a mere shell of herself.

Go to Sleep at a Consistent Time

The consistency in rest patterns will guide you in being able to count on your performance to follow suit. We are creatures of habit. The more routine is implemented into your lifestyle; the rest may benefit from this type of consistency the most. Some like to implement light reading before bed, a melatonin pill, or soft smooth music to help the mind and the body wind down at the same time every night.

Find three different things that you do every night before bed and make sure you do them every time. Create a consistency of rest time on weekends as well. The time can be later, but you should be sure to have a time that you agree with yourself to lay down and get the rest that your academic and athletic performance needs.

Take Naps

Taking short naps is an excellent way to supplement the rest time that you may still need. Any time is a great time to take a nap! In between classes, in between workouts, in the locker room, on the bus, and pretty much anywhere you can safely pull out a pillow. This is a good substitute for caffeinated drinks throughout the day that will make it hard for you to get sleep at night.

Rest and recovery are the key tools that the best in any field understand well. More rest will improve all your physical and mental qualities substantially. If this is an area that you constantly struggle with, look into getting an accountability partner. This is someone that understands your rest schedule and helps you reach your resting goals.

Smartphones and devices today now have rest settings that will aid you in your objective of gaining more rest. Do your research and find out how to use your devices to help you limit your screen time, set alarms, and monitor your rest daily, weekly, and monthly.

A life of mental and physical wear and tear **requires** proper rest. That is the only way that little nagging injuries heal, and the mind truly resets to fight off memory loss, depression, anxiety, and fear.

CHAPTER NINE: A TALE OF TWO TALES

There were two student-athletes. Both athletes held the same position on the basketball team, but their careers had different outcomes.

Bobby Rames (Mr. Blue Collar)

Bobby is the first athlete. Bobby was a red-shirt freshman from a small-town school. He transferred from a junior college. He wasn't highly touted as a recruit. He was under-sized, standing at about 5'9, and had no real intangibles that stood out. Bobby had excellent grades and strong family ties which led to him being accepted into the university academically. The coaches mainly brought him on to raise the team's overall GPA (this happens).

Jojo (The Show)

Jojo is the second athlete, and he is an absolute star. Jojo came in from a very successful junior college program, standing at a solid 6'5. His uncle had a short career in the NBA, and his dad Division I basketball. Jojo was determined to show his new school that he was there to prove himself. In Jojo's junior season at the school, he averaged 25 points per game, 8 assists per game, and 9 rebounds per game. He had not only proven himself but showed he was one of the best that the university had ever seen. Even though, as the season progressed, he constantly split-time with his humble counterpart and red-shirt freshman Bobby Rames. Jojo was inconsistent with things that he was doing off the court.

Preparation Meets Opportunity

Bobby was the trusted piece that gave coaches comfort, trust, and belief that the job would get done. During his redshirt freshman year, Bobby's stat line showed average production (9 points per game, 8 assists, and 1 rebound). Although his statistics wouldn't blow people away, there was one thing that did. Bobby's consistency was unmatched. He would be the first to the locker room and the last to leave the court daily. He also managed to maintain a 3.9 core weighted GPA, while taking some of the most difficult classes afforded to the school.

In the back of Jojo's mind, he always knew that Bobby would cover him. In his irresponsible personal life and lack of proper practice preparation. During the following off-season of the season, something terrible happened. Jojo failed an NCAA drug test leading to an immediate suspension lasting until the foreseeable future.

Outside sources were constantly reaching out to the head coach asking questions like "What's next year going to look like for this upcoming team?", "Who do you think will step up?", "Who do you have coming in to replace JoJo Spiller?". All the while the head coach and the rest of the locker room didn't feel any of that panic. Everyone associated with the program understood that this meant Bobby Rames would be in a prime position to step into his own. The following season was all of what it was supposed to be. Bobby worked all summer developing his craft. He didn't grow at all, he didn't get any faster, but his leadership was tremendous.

The following season Bobby earned all-conference honors, and as years progressed, he became one of the team captains, and was very well respected by his peers. Jojo eventually came back and made a solid contribution, he was never able to play as much as Bobby due to inconsistency in his execution.

Bobby was the same student-athlete the last day of his senior year, as he was the first day of his freshman year. Bobby knew how to execute, and that ultimately made the difference.

Coaches trust executors and will always favor the athletes who show strong discipline.

Discipline: do what you're supposed to do, the way it is supposed to be done, and do it every single time.

There is no cheap way to gain discipline. A person doing what they are supposed to do over 90% will suffocate the opportunity of making mistakes to hurt themselves and their team, out of the equation.

Ditch your ego, and step into your ability to **work hard** and **be consistent**.

When you gain a strong understanding of what your team is trying to do, it will make you much more valuable to your team.

The more value you add, the more people notice, thus making your road to success something that was earned and cannot be taken away.

CLOSING THOUGHTS

The journey that student-athletes embark upon, as it pertains to success, is one not easy to forget. There are things that we learn through this process that we carry with us for the rest of our lives.

Some of the relationships built will be catalysts to the most productive moments in your life, and some of these relationships may guide you into depression and a lack of self-worth. The most important part of the process is to be sure to **never give up.**

Whether you were reading this book from an athlete's point of view, parent of an athlete, friend of an athlete, or someone just looking for an "edge" in life, always remember that nothing that you will ever do will work unless you do.

CPSIA information can be obtained
at www.ICGtesting.com
Printed in the USA
BVHW030619160322
631589BV00004B/34

9 781669 811220